Edexcel Economics A

Theme 1: Introduction to Markets and Market Failure

Helen Coupland-Smith
Carlo Mencattelli

Time2Resources Limited
www.time2resources.co.uk

Published by: Time2Resources Ltd
Orders:
Time2Resources Ltd
PO Box 763
York
YO31 6AA
Tel: 01904 692 924
E-mail: info@time2resources.co.uk
www.time2resources.co.uk

ISBN: 978-1-910769-56-0
Copyright © 2019 Helen Coupland-Smith, Carlo Mencattelli

Printed and typeset by HPE Print, Pickering

This revision guide has been written specifically for the Edexcel Economics A Theme 1: Introduction to Markets and Market Failure unit but has been neither approved nor endorsed by Edexcel. The content remains the responsibility of the authors.

Your Edexcel Economics A Theme 1 Revision Guide

Edexcel Economics A Theme 1:
Introduction to Markets and Market Failure

Name: _____

Start date: _____

Exam dates:

Paper 1 _____

Paper 2 _____

Paper 3 _____

Target grade: _____

Content

About this guide

This guide is designed to carefully cover the whole of the Edexcel Economics A Theme 1: Introduction to Markets and Market Failure. It follows the specification in the correct order and addresses each of the bullet points as given by Edexcel.

To revise means to revisit something you have already done or learnt in order to improve your knowledge. Revision is best done in short but focused sessions and on a regular basis. This handy guide will help you break your revision into short blocks of learning and encourage you to revisit topics and build confidence in exam technique.

As you work through the guide use the traffic lights to record your progress.

Red   You have developed a good understanding of content
- Can select relevant theory to help support an answer

Amber You are able to explain why points made are important
- Develop a line of argument
- Reach a logical conclusion by using theory to address the question

Green   You are confident using economic theory in a range
of real world contexts and to help form supported
judgements
- Able to analyse real economic scenarios in response to extended questio
- Reach justified conclusions

*Tick off each level
reached as you progress
through the sections*

1.1 Nature of Economics

This unit introduces candidates to microeconomics.

Microeconomics:

Whereas Macroeconomics studies the economy as a whole Microeconomics studies **economics on a small scale**. It looks at the **main purpose of economic activity** - the production of goods and services to satisfy the needs and wants of society. This will lead to the improvement of economic welfare for individuals and society as a whole.

The key feature of Microeconomics is that it requires you to have a **good understanding of basic economic models** such as demand and supply and to apply these to empirical or real-world situations. Microeconomics assesses individual markets, price determination and market failure.

In Microeconomics, you will need to acquire knowledge and understanding of the economic problem, how goods and services are allocated in competitive markets, productive efficiency, market failure and how the government intervene in markets to correct market failure. Candidates will need to employ the **economist's tool kit**, making good use of exam technique such as **application, analysis and evaluation** to interpret economic data and written information.

1.1.1 Economics as a Social Science

Economics is a social science. This means that it looks at the way in which people interact and how they behave with each other.

Social sciences such as economics, psychology and sociology involve the study of human beings as individuals and groups and how we interact with each other. Social science is often subject to personal prejudice and is therefore, to some extent, based on opinion.

Natural sciences such as maths, physics and chemistry involve the study of natural events and are objective. They are based on facts provided by the evidence. The laboratory of the natural scientist is one where they can control conditions. Elements of a test are **static** and will always lead to the same result.

The laboratory of the social scientist is one where they cannot control conditions. Elements of a test are **dynamic** and will often lead to different results.

1.1.1 Economics as a Social Science

Thinking like an economist: the process of developing economic models

A model is a theoretical concept that looks at how different variables interact. Economic models will use both qualitative information and statistical data to underpin the theoretical thought process. Models often use empirical (real-world) information to help evidence outcomes. This allows the economist to observe how a change in one variable will impact on other variables.

Assumptions will need to be made:

- Economic agents e.g. individuals and firms are rational and their preferences or choices reflect this

- Consumers wish to maximise utility

- Producers wish to maximise profits

1.1.1 Economics as a Social Science

The use of the ceteris paribus assumption in building models

Ceteris paribus means 'all other factors remain the same'. The study of Economics is like working in a laboratory. When Economists raise the price of a good or service they make the assumption that other factors e.g. consumer incomes do not change. This allows us to identify the impact of changes in one variable e.g. price on a second variable such as demand.

The economist will try to create conditions under which a change in one variable will lead to a change in a second variable by using the ceteris paribus principle. For example, we might state that ceteris paribus, an increase in the price of bananas would lead to a decrease in their demand. If other factors were to change e.g. a new report showing previously unknown life enhancing properties of bananas then this might not be the case. A rise in the price of bananas could occur at the same time as an increase in demand.

1.1.2 Positive and Normative Economic Statements

Positive statements are objective, factually based comments that can be tested. They are not influenced by the opinion or prejudice of people. They allow scientific testing to take place that can be accepted or rejected. For example, the unemployment rate is 8% is a positive statement because it is based on factual evidence.

Normative statements are subjective, questionable comments that are difficult to test. They are influenced by the opinion or prejudice of people. For example, the government should increase spending to help reduce the unemployment rate. Normative statements require **value judgements**.

The role of value judgements in influencing decision making and policy
A value judgment is a statement that has been put forward by an individual that cannot be verified factually. Value judgements influence economic decision-making and policy. Economic agents have to choose between alternative options, for every decision made there is an opportunity cost.

1.1.2 Positive and Normative Economic Statements

Basing decision-making on positive statements is likely to lead to certain outcomes e.g. increasing the price of a normal good will reduce demand. However, the future, by definition, is uncertain. This means that choices have to be made that will lead to uncertain outcomes. Economic decision-making and policy is based on both positive statements and value judgements.

People's views concerning the best option are influenced by:

- the positive consequences of different decisions
  - This will depend on the subjective nature of the outcome
  - Normative statements are based on value judgements and it is not always easy to clearly see whether one option is better than another
- moral and political judgements
  - The best option for an individual may differ from that of the best option for society as a whole
  - The extent to which self-interest is the best way to meet the needs of society is an emotive subject

1.1.1 Economic Methodology

1. Explain why economics is classed as a social science.

2. Explain what is meant by a natural science.

3. What is the main purpose of economic activity?

4. What is meant by an economic model?

5. State one objective of a consumer and one objective of a producer.

1.1.1 Economic Methodology

6. What is meant by microeconomics?

7. What is meant by the ceteris paribus principle?

8. Distinguish between positive and normative statements.

9. With the use of an example explain what is meant by a value judgement.

10. Explain how people's views of the best economic options are influenced by moral and political judgements.

Tick off each level reached as you progress through the sections

1.1.3 The Economic Problem

Economic activity: all actions involved in the production, distribution and consumption of goods and services in order to satisfy needs and wants.

The central purpose of **economic activity** is the production of goods and services to satisfy **needs** and **wants**. Economic activity will improve **economic welfare**, the benefit gained by individuals, firms or society.

- **Needs** are those things required that are essential to maintain survival
- **Wants** are those things that are desired but not essential to survival

People have unlimited wants. However, there aren't enough resources available to supply all of these wants. This creates the economic problem of **scarcity**. The 'economic problem' occurs when there are **finite resources** available to supply **infinite** or **unlimited wants** i.e. scarcity.

Therefore, **choices** have to be made about how to use these scarce resources.

1.1.3 The Economic Problem

The **economic problem** tries to answer 3 basic questions:

What to produce?

- Economic incentives will provide **economic agents** with the information required to tell them what goods and services to produce

- **Economic agents** are the individuals and firms that partake in economic activity i.e. the demand for and supply of goods and services

How to produce?

- Firms will combine the **factors of production** in order to produce a good or a service

- The **factors of production are** land, labour, capital and enterprise

Who to produce for?

- In a **free market economy** (or market economy) goods and services are produced according to demand and supply. If there is demand for a product a firm may wish to supply it for a profit

- A **free market economy** is one where firms decide what goods and services to produce with limited intervention from the government

1.1.3 The Economic Problem

Renewable resources are ones that can be replenished e.g. trees can be used for wood to generate fuel but they can be replanted. Sustainable resources are ones that are being used for economic activities in such a manner that they will not run out. However, they must be used sensibly e.g. not over fishing and replanting trees.

Non-renewable resources are ones that are in finite supply and therefore will run out e.g. oil or natural gas.

The environment is a scarce resource, as much of what we use up in economic activity is non-renewable. Therefore, we need to use these resources in a sustainable manner. Exploitation of land has led to serious environmental problems:

- Resource depletion as non-renewable resources are being exploited

- Resource degradation as the use of resources impacts negatively on the quality of life e.g. pollution and the destruction of habitat, wildlife and cultures on a global scale

1.1.3 Economic Resources

Opportunity cost: the benefit lost of the next best alternative when making a choice.

- As all resources are scarce choices must be made in order to allocate these resources

- There are always competing alternatives when making choices e.g. should I buy a Pepsi or a Fanta?

- If I buy a Fanta I have lost the benefit of the closest alternative, a Pepsi

- There is an opportunity cost for all decisions made by economic agents

Opportunity cost is a very important concept in Economics. Economic agents such as individuals, firms and governments are constantly making choices.

. . . .
Examiner's tip: In the examination, you will have to analyse the choices available to economic agents based on the evidence presented. Remember the need to use economic terminology such as opprtunity cost to unerpin your answers.

1.1.3 Economic Resources

Opportunity cost is important in all decisions made by economic agents.

Economic incentives will provide economic agents with the information required to tell them what goods and services to produce. Producers and government will supply goods and services that are demanded by consumers.

Consumers will want to maximise their utility or satisfaction. They will therefore choose goods or services that maximise their utility.

Producers will look to maximise profits. They will combine the factors of production (land, labour, capital and entrepreneurship) in order to produce goods or services that achieve this.

Government will look to maximise the welfare of its citizens. They will commit government spending to areas that will best do this.

1.1.3 Economic Resources

1. What is meant by the economic problem?

2. Distinguish between unlimited wants and finite resources.

3. What is meant by scarcity?

4. What is the impact of scarcity on choices?

5. What is meant by opportunity cost?

6. Why do choices have an opportunity cost?

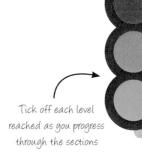

Tick off each level reached as you progress through the sections

1.1.4 Production Possibility Frontiers

Production possibility: the maximum possible combination of output of two products e.g. good x and good y that an economy can produce given the current resources available.
Production possibility frontier (PPF): a diagram that is used to show the different combinations of output for two products given the resources available.

- As the output of good x increases that of good y decreases and vice versa

- The PPF illustrates the problem of choosing how to use scarce resources when producing goods and services

- There is an opportunity cost in deciding what combinations of good x and good y to produce

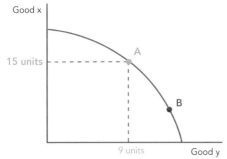

At point A the business can produce 15 units of good x and 9 units of good y.

The business can produce a combination of good x and good y anywhere along the PPF e.g. point B.

1.1.4 Production Possibility Frontiers

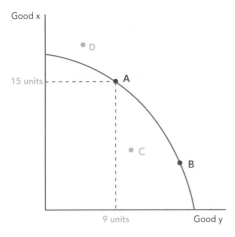

Good x

15 units

9 units

Good y

• D

A

• C

B

Producing anywhere along the PPF shows a full use of resources e.g. **points A** and **B**. All factors of production are being used and there is no unemployment of resources.

Therefore, there is an **efficient allocation of resources**.

Producing anywhere within the PPF shows under-use of resources e.g. point C. More resources could be used if there was an increase in efficiency. At point C the country could produce more of both good x and good y without affecting the current output of these products. Therefore, there is an **inefficient allocation of resources**.

Point D is **unobtainable** as there are not enough resources to produce this level of output. Production at all points on, or within the frontier, are **possible**.

1.1.4 Production Possibility Frontiers

The PPF can be used to show the concepts of scarcity, choice and opportunity cost:
- By choosing good x the economic agent sacrifices the benefit of using good y
- Due to resources being scarce a choice has had to be made between two competing uses
- This shows that the basic economic problem is due to infinite wants but finite resources

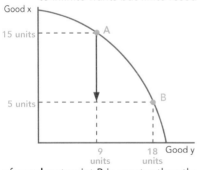

At point A 15 units of **good x** are being produced and 9 units of **good y**. At point B 5 units of **good x** are being produced and 18 units of **good y**. Therefore in order to allocate resources to produce 9 additional units of **good y** a business has had to sacrifice 10 units of output of **good x**. The opportunity cost of 9 more units of **good y** is 10 units of **good x**.

The opportunity cost of increasing production of **good y** will be higher, the more is produced. Therefore, the opportunity cost of producing more of **good y** at point B is greater than that at point A. This is because the gradient of the PPF is **concave** i.e. becoming steeper showing more and more units of **good x** need to be given up to produce the same amount of **good y**.

1.1.4 Production Possibility Frontiers

An increase in **economic growth** can be caused by an increase in factor inputs e.g. immigration will see a growth of labour as an input so that we can produce more. Increased production of investment goods will allow us to produce more goods and services in the future.

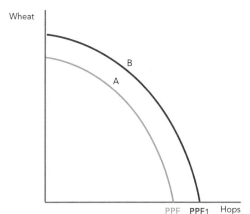

Economic growth caused by an increase in factors of production available in an economy can cause the PPF to shift outwards and to the right.

This will result in an increase in the productive capacity of the economy from PPF to PPF1 i.e. greater output can be produced..

1.1.4 Production Possibility Frontiers

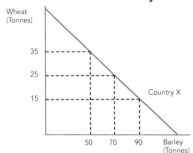

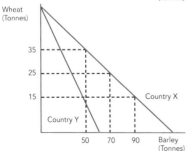

Marginal analysis can be used to enhance our understanding of the production possibility frontier. Marginal analysis looks at the opportunity cost between two goods shown on the PPF. For a straight line PPF the opportunity cost between two products is always constant. Country X can produce a combination of wheat and barley. If it produces 35 tonnes of wheat it can produce 50 tonnes of barley. If the country reduces its output of wheat by 10 tonnes it can increase its output of barley by 20 tonnes. If it were to reduce its output further to 15 tonnes it can increase production of barley to 90 tonnes. The opportunity cost of 20 tonnes of barley is 10 tonnes of wheat.

The steeper the PPF the greater the opportunity cost. In the diagram the opportunity cost of 10 tonnes of wheat for country X is 20 tonnes of barley. However, the opportunity cost for country Y is only 10 tonnes of barley.

1.1.4 Production Possibility Frontiers

A PPF can be used to distinguish between capital (investment) goods and consumer (consumption) goods.

- **Capital goods** are those that produce a stream of income in the future e.g. machinery

- **Consumer goods** are those that produce an immediate benefit to the consumer e.g. a car for personal use

Conflicting objectives might arise as there is an opportunity cost as to what goods and services to produce. It might be in the interests of suppliers to produce investment goods i.e. those that produce a stream of income in the future. Consumers might wish to see a greater supply of consumption goods i.e. those that produce a benefit today.

1.1.4 Production Possibility Frontiers

1. All points on a PPF show which **one** of the following?
   a. Full use of resources
   b. All firms benefitting from economies of scale
   c. Equal income distribution in an economy
   d. Spare capacity in the economy

2. A shift to the right of an economy's PPF shows which **one** of the following?
   a. A fall in the efficiency of factors of production
   b. An increase in the utilisation of factors of production
   c. An increase in the productive capacity of the economy
   d. An increase in the production of one product at the expense of another

3. A country operating within its PPF shows which **one** of the following?
   a. Under-utilisation of resources
   b. A fall in productive capacity
   c. Overtime being worked by labour
   d. A shift to the left of the PPF

1.1.4 Production Possibility Frontiers

4. Draw and label a PPF diagram showing consumer goods on the Y axis and capital goods on the X axis. Show what will happen if there is an increase in the productivity of the production of consumer goods.

5. Draw and label a PPF diagram with wine on the X axis and cheese on the Y axis. Along the PPF create four points A, B, C and D.
   Use the diagram to explain why increasing the production of cheese will lead to an increasing opportunity cost.

6. Explain why the opportunity costs for a linear and concave PPF curve are different.

7. Draw and label a PPF for an economy showing the relationship between public goods and private goods. Annotate the middle point of the PPF as point A. Explain why an increase in the production of private goods will lead to a reduction in the output of public goods.

8. Draw and label a PPF diagram showing point A within the PPF, points B and C on the PPF and point D outside of the PPF. Explain each point on the diagram.

Tick off each level reached as you progress through the sections

1.1.5 Specialisation and the Division of Labour

Specialisation: economic units such as individuals, firms, regions or countries concentrate on producing specific goods or services.

In *The Wealth of Nations* (1776), Scottish Economist, Adam Smith looked at the concept of the division of labour. Through specialisation, breaking down large tasks into smaller components, each worker becomes a specialist, and therefore better at their job. This leads to improved efficiency and productivity.

Specialised use of workers within an organisation is called the division of labour. Specialisation is likely to lead to increased output per worker i.e. greater labour productivity as the workforce have a better understanding of their job roles. This will help to address the problem of scarcity as there will be a greater supply of goods and services to meet unlimited wants.

Specialisation increases output as economic units become more effective and efficient in what they produce due to:
- Greater understanding of the requirements of production
- Each economic unit can specialise in what they are best at
- Efficient use of time as there is no switching between tasks
- Technical economies of scale as capital equipment is used to produce goods and services

1.1.5 Specialisation and the Division of Labour

However, there are disadvantages in using specialisation and division of labour in organising production:

- Work can become monotonous
  - This can affect quality and productivity
  - Can increase absenteeism
- May be limited by the size of the market
  - Small firms cannot afford to introduce specialisation
- Threat of structural unemployment if an industry goes into decline
- Reduces flexibility of the workforce
  - Production flows may be stopped affecting the ability to meet demand

1.1.5 Specialisation and the Division of Labour

Specialisation and the division of labour allow an economic agent such as a firm to trade by:

- Reducing unit costs e.g. through bulk buying
- Improving quality e.g. through better training and skills
- Using technology to increase speed and improve accuracy e.g. production lines
- Creating a unique selling point by producing better quality
- Countries, regions, firms and individuals will specialise to benefit from these advantages.
- This enables trade with other economic agents that have specialised in different fields
- The production possibility frontier will shift outwards

However, specialisation can have serious repercussions as economic agents that specialise are at the risk of losing their markets. In a competitive global market UK economic agents can quickly lose market share. This means that the UK must continually strive to improve production processes. A focus on highly differentiated products such as financial services and premium cars has allowed the UK to develop new industries whilst old ones such as textiles have declined.

1.1.5 Specialisation and the Division of Labour

Increased output from specialisation can be exchanged for other goods and services that the economic unit is not as good at producing. Specialisation therefore allows for the exchange of goods and services between the economic units.

The effective exchange of goods and services necessitates an efficient means of exchange. In earlier times a **barter** system was used to exchange goods and services. Barter occurs when goods and services are exchanged for other goods and services between two parties. This happens without a formal medium of exchange such as money. However, the use of barter caused a number of problems in the exchange process.

Many of these problems have been overcome by the use of **money**. Money is anything that is generally accepted in exchange for goods and services. Money is more efficient than barter as it acts as:

- A medium of exchange - an intermediary between two parties when buying and selling
- A measure of value - it allows us to measure the value of goods and services in units e.g. the prices of goods and services
- A store of value - it can be kept for future use
- A standard of deferred payment - it allows us to pay for goods and services provided now at a later date

1.1.5 Specialisation and the Division of Labour

1. Define the term specialisation.

2. Define the term division of labour.

3. State three reasons why specialisation can help to increase output at a firm.

4. State three disadvantages to using specialisation and the division of labour in organising production.

5. Explain two reasons why specialisation and the division of labour allow an economic agent such as a firm to trade.

1.1.5 Specialisation and the Division of Labour

6. Explain two advantages to a country of specialisation.

7. Explain two disadvantages to a country of specialisation.

8. Why is the use of money, as a means of exchanging goods and services important if a business is to specialise and use the division of labour?

9. Which three of the following can improve labour productivity?

   a. Increasing the amount of labour available

   b. Using more capital equipment

   c. Specialisation

   d. Training

Tick off each level reached as you progress through the sections

1.1.6 Free market economies, mixed economy and command economy

In a **free market** the basic economic problem of what to produce, how to produce and for whom to produce is solved by **market forces**. This means that the forces of supply and demand work together to determine what price and quantity of goods and services are supplied. Businesses will supply what is demanded at a price that allows them to make a profit. Customers will demand what is supplied if it is at a price that they can afford. This is known as the **market mechanism**.

- Consumers will act to maximise their personal welfare

- Producers will act to maximise their profits

- Owners of factor inputs will act to maximise personal gain:

  - Land – rent

  - Capital – interest

  - Labour – remuneration

  - Enterprise – profit

- Government will act to maximise the benefits to society

1.1.6 Free market economies, mixed economy and command economy

Free market economies have a number of characteristics:

- private sector ownership
- free enterprise i.e. demand and supply is determined by the market mechanism
- limited government intervention
- firms compete for market share
- society competes for employment and salaries
- allocation of resources is determined by market forces

Adam Smith wrote about an 'invisible hand' that self-regulated the behaviour of the market place. Through this, individuals seeking to maximise personal gains will lead to an efficient allocation of resources. This self-interest benefits society as a whole.

'It is not from the benevolence of the butcher, the brewer, or the baker, that we expect our dinner, but from their regard to their own interest. We address ourselves, not to their humanity but to their self-love, and never talk to them of our own necessities but of their advantages.'

The Wealth of Nations, 1776

1.1.6 Free market economies, mixed economy and command economy

Classical economists suggest a **laissez-faire** (to leave alone) approach by the government towards markets. This will provide the greatest good for the greatest number of people.

There are a number of advantages and disadvantages to free market economies.

Advantages of free markets	Disadvantages of free markets
Competitive market	Inequalities in wealth
Consumer choice	Inequality in incomes
Rewards entrepreneurship	Provision of demerit goods
Encourages innovation	Less provision of merit goods
Productive efficiency	Little regulation
Economic growth	Less support for the vulnerable

1.1.6 Free market economies, mixed economy and command economy

Friedrich August (F.A.) von Hayek (1899-1992) was a famous free market Austrian economist. He became a British subject in 1938 and worked at the London School of Economics (LSE).

He believed that the state should not interfere in the free market and that its role should be to maintain the rule of law. He argued against collectivism, where economic activities were centrally planned, particularly by government. He believed that this form of government intervention eventually led to totalitarian rule with a one-party government restricting freedoms and undermining democracy. Therefore, decentralisation and decision making should be left in the hands of individuals and groups of individuals e.g. businesses.

Hayek believed that the state had a role to play in creating a 'safety net' such as social insurance e.g. the National Health Service to support workers in times of need e.g. unemployment. However, too much government intervention made problems worse and distorted the smooth running of the free market mechanism.

1.1.6 Free market economies, mixed economy and command economy

A **command economy** occurs when resources, including labour, are allocated by the government. Rationing and planning take place and the state decides what, how and for whom to produce. This can lead to greater equality and the removal of demerit goods from the economy.

Karl Marx (1818-1883) was a German economist who believed that labour was exploited by capitalists, the owners of the means of production e.g. factories.

In his 1867 book, Das Kapital, Marx suggested that labour was underpaid by the owners of businesses, which enabled them to make profits. Eventually, as businesses grow in order to become more efficient ownership is in the hands of a few wealthy capitalists and there is a mass of poor underpaid labour. His works have had an enormous impact on our history e.g. Communist governments in Russia and China.

1.1.6 Free market economies, mixed economy and command economy

Marx and Karl Engels published the **Communist Manifesto** in 1848. It had far reaching effects on the 20th Century. It led to revolution in Russia and China:

'Workers of the World, Unite. You have nothing to lose but your chains'

Marx believed that exploitation of the labour force lead to a class struggle which would lead to the rise, fall and ultimate destruction of capitalism.

Capitalism would exploit workers and create an underpaid proletariat who did not benefit from the economic system. The only material value they possessed was their labour. Ultimately, the capitalists would be overthrown.

This would lead to **socialism**, where the means of production is owned by central authorities and workers are paid wages and can choose how to spend their money.

Finally comes the formation of **communism** where the community of people (government) own the means of production and there is no need to exploit labour as workers share output distributed centrally.

1.1.6 Free market economies, mixed economy and command economy

A **mixed economy** occurs when resources are allocated by a combination of both the market mechanism (free market) and the government (command or planned economy).

Enterprise is actively encouraged but the government will act to:

- Reduce negative externalities
- Provide public goods
- Control demerit goods
- Supply merit goods

In a mixed economy the role of the state is important. It provides public goods e.g. infrastructure and defence; controls macroeconomic variables e.g. inflation; reduces negative externalities, provides a legal framework e.g. intellectual property rights, encourages free trade e.g. restrict monopoly power and regulates markets to reduce consumer exploitation and create competition.

1.1.6 Free market economies, mixed economy and command economy

1. State four characteristics of free market economies.

2. Explain why Adam Smith believed that self-interest would benefit society as a whole.

3. State three advantages of free market economies.

4. State three disadvantages of free market economies.

5. Explain why Hayek believed that government had a role to play in an economy.

6. Define a free market economy.

1.1.6 Free market economies, mixed economy and command economy

7. Define a command economy.

8. Explain how, according to Marx, capitalism would lead to socialism.

9. Explain how, according to Marx, socialism would lead to communism.

10. Define a mixed market economy.

11. State three roles of the state in a mixed market economy.

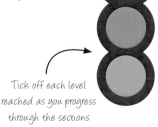

Tick off each level reached as you progress through the sections

1.2.1 Rational decision making

Rational economic decision making occurs when economic agents make logical decisions to improve their satisfaction or achieve the greatest benefit, given the available choices.

Maximisation occurs when an economic agent tries to obtain the most that they can from the economic activity that they undertake.

This will differ dependent on the economic agent:

- Households or consumers wish to maximise their **utility** or personal satisfaction
- Firms wish to maximise their **profits**
- Government wish to maximise the **welfare** of the population

Achieving economic objectives requires the use of resources in order to meet the goals of an economic agent over a period of time.

The economic objectives of **households** might include:

- The maximisation of private benefit from consumption

Individuals will seek to attain the highest level of satisfaction available in their consumption of goods and services.

1.2.1 Rational decision making

- The maximisation of private benefit from working

Individuals will seek to attain the highest benefit available in the supply of their labour. This might include higher pay or better working conditions.

The economic objectives of **firms** might include:

- Profit maximisation

Firms will seek to attain the highest level of profit available in the production of goods and services.

- Profit satisficing

A level of profit below profit maximisation that satisfies the needs of the owners or managers of an organisation e.g. working fewer hours to enjoy more leisure time or behaving ethically.

- Sales maximisation

Some firms will seek to sell as much as possible, perhaps to gain market share.

- Growth

Some firms seek to maximise their growth potential e.g. through the takeover of other firms.

1.2.2 Demand

Demand: the amount of a good or service a consumer or group of consumers are willing and able to buy at a set price at a given point in time.

A **normal good** is one where if price rises demand will fall and vice versa i.e. a negative correlation.

Rational choice theory makes the assumption that all individuals make logical decisions that will maximise their personal benefit i.e. self-interest.

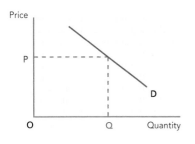

The relationship between price and quantity demanded can be shown using a **demand curve**.

The demand curve shows the quantity demanded for a good, at any given price, over a period of time.

- As price falls quantity demanded rises
- As price rises quantity demanded falls

1.2.2 Demand

A change in price is always shown by a **movement along** the demand curve.

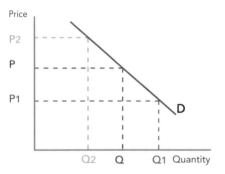

At price **P** the quantity demanded is **Q**.

If the price falls from **P** to **P1** the quantity demanded rises from **Q** to **Q1**.

If the price rises from **P** to **P2** the quantity demanded falls from **Q** to **Q2**.

Ceteris paribus means all other factors remain the same. The demand curve is based on the assumption that all other factors remain the same e.g. consumer incomes do not change. This allows for the identification of the impact in changes of one factor e.g. price.

1.2.2 Demand

There are a number of **determinants** or **factors** influencing the level of demand. The quantity demanded of a good or service is said to be a function of all of these factors. This can be shown mathematically:

- qd = f (p, y, p of other goods/services, consumer tastes, all other factors)
  - *qd = quantity demanded*
  - *f = is a function of*
  - *p = price*
  - *y = consumer income*

The price of the good (p)

A **normal good** is one where:

If the price of the good or service increases demand for that good or service will decrease.

If the price of the good or service decreases demand for that good or service will increase.

A **Veblen good**, named after American Economist Thorstein Veblen, identified a **'snob effect'** where people paid more for certain products as their price increased. He believed that this was due to the increased status that buying higher priced goods conferred on the buyer. This would be classed as an **abnormal good**.

1.2.2 Demand

Consumer income (y)
As incomes of consumers increases demand for normal goods will increase. If consumer incomes fall demand will also fall i.e. there is a positive correlation between income and demand.

An **inferior good** is one where demand decreases as incomes increase. As the consumer has more income they substitute inferior goods with better quality goods that they can now afford.

Economist Sir Robert Giffen identified certain inferior products where demand rose as consumer incomes increased. Alfred Marshall called these products Giffen goods. Giffen suggested, for example, that a rise in the price of bread meant that poor Irish families could no longer afford more expensive products such as meat. Therefore, they spent even more of their income on bread.

Wealth
The stock of assets held by individuals will impact on demand. As the value of stock increases e.g. housing and shares people will feel more confident to spend as their assets will be worth more. In addition, banks are more likely to provide loans against the increased value of the assets. This will lead a rightward shift in the demand curve.

1.2.2 Demand

Prices of other goods and services

Substitute products are those that act as an alternative for consumers and therefore create competition. If the price of good A increases the demand for good B will increase e.g. Coca-Cola and Pepsi Cola.

Complementary products are those that are often bought alongside each other. If the price of good A increases the demand for good B will decrease e.g. fish and chips.

Individual preferences

People's tastes change over time and demand for fashionable products changes regularly, often manipulated by advertising. As some products become more fashionable there is an increase in demand. Just as quickly, demand can disappear as tastes and fashion change.

Social and emotional factors

Social factors can influence consumer choice as demographics change. This might be caused by immigration, an ageing society or changes in technology. People like to 'fit in' and will follow social conventions or 'norms'. Peer group pressure has a significant impact on decision making. Emotional factors depend on our psychological state. A feel good factor might see increased demand for certain products such as holidays whilst depression can lead to increased demand for alcohol and drugs.

1.2.2 Demand

If the change in demand is caused by any factor other than price then the demand curve **shifts**.

At price **P** the quantity demanded is **Q**.

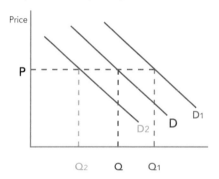

If a change in a variable other than price causes an **increase** in demand the demand curve shifts **right** from **D** to **D1** and quantity demanded increases from **Q** to **Q1**.

If a change in a variable other than price causes a **decrease** in demand the demand curve shifts **left** from **D** to **D2** and quantity demanded decreases from **Q** to **Q2**.

1.2.2 Demand

Utility theory is concerned with the satisfaction that an individual derives from consuming a good or service. The unit of measurement for utility is called **utils**.

Marginal utility is the amount of satisfaction an individual derives from consuming one extra unit of a good or service. **Total utility** is the aggregate amount of satisfaction an individual derives from consuming a good or service. **Total utility** diminishes or decreases over time. As individuals increase consumption of a good or service the amount of satisfaction, or utils, that they receive from this consumption will decline. This occurs as an individual becomes more **satiated**, or satisfied, with the product.

SOFT DRINKS	TOTAL UTILITY (Utils)
0	0
1	20
2	36
3	44
4	44
5	32

Total utility can be illustrated in a table. A consumer gains 20 utils of satisfaction from consuming 1 soft drink. The satisfaction, or utility, gained from the second soft drink is less than the first, but total utility increases to 36. At some point, e.g. the 4th drink, there is no additional satisfaction. After this point utility starts to fall and there is **dissatisfaction** from consuming an extra unit. Presumably the individual would not consume this final unit. However, there is evidence that this happens in the real world. As consumption increases, total utility rises at first and then starts to diminish.

1.2.2 Demand

Total utility can be illustrated graphically. As consumption increases, total utility rises at first and then starts to diminish.

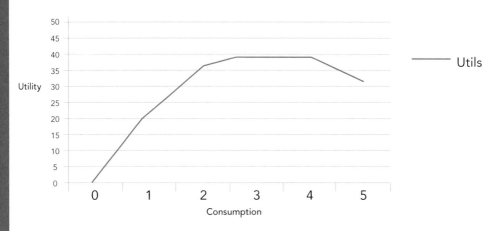

1.2.2 Demand

The **margin** is fundamental when individuals make choices. Individuals will only choose an option if the MB > MC. This will improve TU. If MC is greater than MB then TU will actually fall and the individual would experience dissatisfaction from consuming the extra unit. The individual will consume up to the point where MB equals MC. Marginal utility is shown by the formula:

Marginal utility
Change in number of units consumed

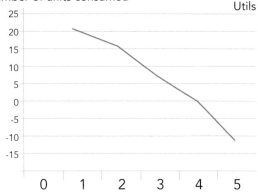

SOFT DRINKS	TOTAL UTILITY (Utils)	MARGINAL UTILITY (Utils)
0	0	
1	20	20
2	36	16
3	44	8
4	44	0
5	32	-12

1.2.2 Demand

Diminishing marginal utility and the demand curve.

As consumption increases, marginal utility diminishes giving us **diminishing marginal utility**.

If increased consumption of a good or service provides fewer and fewer amounts of marginal utility, then at some point, consumers will only buy additional units if its price falls. Therefore, we can equate diminishing marginal utility to the demand curve. As price falls, consumers gain greater satisfaction from demanding the good. This means that as price falls, demand increases. As price increases, demand falls.

Marginal utility and opportunity cost

Opportunity cost can be used to look at utility. If an individual gains greater marginal utility from product A than product B this will be reflected in the opportunity cost and they will choose an extra unit of product A rather than product B. This suggests that they prefer product A as the benefit foregone of the next best alternative i.e. product B is lesser.

Test Yourself

1.2.1 Rational decision making and 1.2.2 Demand

1. Define the term rational economic decision making.

2. Define the term "demand".

3. Distinguish between a "normal good" and an "inferior good".

4. What is the relationship between quantity demanded and price for a normal good?

5. What happens to demand for an inferior good as incomes increase?

6. With the use of appropriate diagrams explain what happens to demand if:

   - Prices rise
   - Prices fall
   - Demand increases as a result of a change in any variable other than price
   - Demand decreases as a result of a change in any variable other than price

1.2.1 Rational decision making and 1.2.2 Demand

7. List four factors that influence the demand for a good or service.

8. What is the relationship between two products that are substitutes of each other?

9. What is the relationship between two products that are complements of each other?

10. Distinguish between total and marginal utility.

11. Explain why the hypothesis of diminishing marginal utility supports a downward sloping demand curve.

Tick off each level reached as you progress through the sections

1.2.3 Price, income and cross elasticities of demand

Elasticity theory looks at the responsiveness of one variable in relationship to another.

Percentage change is calculated using the formula: $\dfrac{\text{Change in value} \times 100}{\text{Original value}}$

Elasticity coefficient: the measure of the responsiveness of one variable to change in another.

- If price increases by 5% demand might decrease by 15%
- The elasticity coefficient is given by -15%/+5% = -3

> For example:
> If price changes from £1.20 to £1.26
> Change in value = £1.20 (original value) to £1.26 (new value) = £0.06 (change in value)
> $\dfrac{£0.06}{£1.20} \times 100 = 5\%$

In elasticity theory the + and − sign are used to show the relationship between two variables:

- A **+ sign** stands for a **positive** relationship e.g. if income increases (+) demand increases (+)
- A **− sign** stands for a **negative** relationship e.g. if price increases (+) demand decreases (-)

1.2.3 Price, income and cross elasticities of demand

Price elasticity of demand (PED): measures the responsiveness of demand to a change in price.

Calculated using the formula: Percentage change in quantity demanded
                                Percentage change in price

Or: $$\frac{\% \Delta \text{ qd}}{\% \Delta \text{ p}}$$

> For example:
> Price goes down by 10% leading to a 15% rise in demand
> 15%/-10% = -1.5 PED = -1.5

If the PED coefficient is less than -1 e.g. -1.5 then the product is price elastic.
Price elastic: a change in price will lead to a more than proportional change in demand.

If the PED coefficient is greater than -1 e.g. -0.8 then the product is price inelastic.
Price inelastic: a change in price will lead to a less than proportional change in demand.

1.2.3 Price, income and cross elasticities of demand

Price elastic demand

A price elastic product will have a PED coefficient between -1 and infinity (∞). If price was to change the quantity demanded would change by a greater amount. Therefore, a firm should look to lower price. This would lead to higher sales revenue.

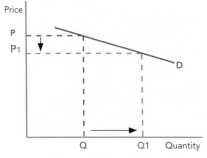

- an increase in **P** will lead to a decrease in D and a decrease in total revenue (TR)

- a decrease in **P** will lead to an increase in D and an increase in total revenue (TR)

The shallower the gradient of the demand curve the greater the level of elasticity.

A **perfectly elastic** product will have a PED coefficient of ∞. If price was to change the quantity demanded would be infinite. In theory, the firm could not increase price as there would be no demand. This is shown by a horizontal demand curve.

1.2.3 Price, income and cross elasticities of demand

Price inelastic demand
A price inelastic product will have a PED coefficient between 0 and -1. If price was to change the quantity demanded would change by a lesser amount. Therefore, a firm should look to raise price. This would lead to higher sales revenue.

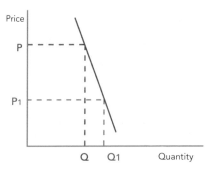

- an increase in **P** will lead to a decrease in **D** and an increase in TR

- a decrease in **P** will lead to an increase in **D** and a decrease in TR

The steeper the gradient of the demand curve the greater the level of inelasticity.

A **perfectly inelastic** product will have a PED coefficient of 0. If price was to change the quantity demanded would not be affected. In theory, the firm could charge as high a price as it wanted. This is shown by a vertical demand curve.

1.2.3 Price, income and cross elasticities of demand

In the exam you can be asked to calculate PED.

Worked example: A firm sells 100 units at a price of £10.00 per unit. It raises price by £5.00 and demand falls to 90 units.	
% $\triangle$ qd	% $\triangle$ p
change in value/original value x 100	change in value/original value x 100
(100 – 90) / 100	(£10.00 – £15.00) / 100
-10/100 x 100	+£5.00/£10.00 x 100
-10%	+50%
% $\triangle$ qd = -10 = -0.2 PED coefficient is -0.2 and is therefore inelastic % $\triangle$ p +50	
What would happen to total revenue? 100 units at £10 = total revenue of 100 x £10.00 = £1000 90 units at £15 = total revenue of 90 x £15.00 = £1350 Raising the price of a price inelastic good has led to a less than proportional change in demand and hence total revenue has increased.	

1.2.3 Price, income and cross elasticities of demand

Price elasticity of demand is determined by:

Availability of substitutes
- The number and closeness of available **substitutes** will help to determine PED
- If there are no close or lack of available substitutes the product is likely to be very price inelastic and vice versa

Time
- In the **short run** products are likely to be more price inelastic as consumers find it difficult to change their shopping habits
- In the **long run** products are likely to be more price elastic as consumers adjust to changing market conditions

Definition of the market
- As we widen the market PED becomes more inelastic e.g. cigarettes are very price inelastic as there are no close substitutes
- However, the demand for specific brands of cigarette will have a higher PED

1.2.3 Price, income and cross elasticities of demand

Income elasticity of demand (YED): measures the responsiveness of demand to a change in income.

Calculated using the formula: Percentage change in quantity demanded
                                 Percentage change in income

Or: $\frac{\% \Delta \text{ qd}}{\% \Delta \text{ y}}$

> For example:
> Income goes up by 3% leading to a 6% rise in demand.
> +6%/+3% = +2 YED = +2

Income elastic: a change in income will lead to a more than proportional change in demand.

Income inelastic: a change in income will lead to a less than proportional change in demand.

If the YED coefficient is greater than +1 or less than -1 then the product is income elastic.

If the YED coefficient is between -1 and +1 then the product is income inelastic.

The YED of a normal good will always be positive whereas the YED of an inferior good will be negative.

1.2.3 Price, income and cross elasticities of demand

Income elasticity of demand is determined by:
Whether the good is a necessity or a luxury

- At higher standards of living increased consumer incomes see additional demand tend towards luxury goods as demand for necessities is satiated

- **Necessities** are products that have a positive YED that is between 0 and 1

- **Luxuries** are products that have a positive YED that is greater than 1

The level of income of a consumer

- Poorer consumers tend to spend their income on **necessities**

- As they become wealthier the YED for necessities moves towards zero as consumers are satisfied with the amount of the product e.g. staple foods that they can buy

- **Normal goods** that are necessities will have lower positive YED coefficients

- As consumer incomes increase they are likely to spend some of their income on **luxuries**. These products e.g. cars and foreign holidays will have a higher positive YED

1.2.3 Price, income and cross elasticities of demand

Standards of living

- Wealthier countries are likely to have consumers with higher disposable incomes

- This means that they have greater spending power and are likely to use some of this greater income to buy luxury goods and services

- Therefore, firms will produce superior products that meet the needs of these consumers e.g. high technology goods and complex financial services

The economic cycle

- When the economy is in recovery mode and leading into boom disposable incomes increase and consumers spend a greater proportion of this increase in income firstly on necessities and then on luxury goods

- When the economy is in decline and leading into slump disposable incomes decrease and consumers spend a lesser proportion of their incomes on luxury goods, moving to necessities and then inferior goods

1.2.3 Price, income and cross elasticities of demand

It is important to understand the **key relationships** studied in this unit so far:

- The relationship between **price elasticity of demand** and a **firm's total revenue** or **consumer's total expenditure**

  - A **rise** in the price of a **price inelastic good** will see an **increase in total revenue** for the firm and **total expenditure** of consumers

  - **A fall** in the price of a **price inelastic good** will see a **decrease in total revenue** for the firm and **total expenditure** of consumers

  - The **inverse** of this rule is true for **price elastic goods**

  - If total revenue or total consumer expenditure does not change when price changes the good has **unitary elasticity**

- The relationship between **income elasticity of demand** and **normal** and **inferior goods**

  - A **normal good** is one where an **increase in income** leads to a **rise in demand**, whilst a **decrease in income reduces demand**

  - An **inferior good** is one where an **increase in income reduces demand**, whilst a **decrease in income** leads to a **rise in demand**

1.2.3 Price, income and cross elasticities of demand

Cross-elasticity of demand (XED): measures the responsiveness of demand for one good, x to a change in price of another good, y.

Calculated using the formula: Percentage change in quantity demanded of good x
                                  Percentage change in price of good y

Or: $\dfrac{\% \Delta qdx}{\% \Delta py}$

For example:
The price of good y increases by 10%, this leads to an increase in the demand for good x of 5%.
+5%/+10% = +0.5 XED = +0.5

Cross elastic: a change in price of good x will lead to a more than proportional change in demand of good y.
Cross inelastic: a change in price of good x will lead to a less than proportional change in demand of good y.
If the XED coefficient is greater than +1 or less than -1 then the product is cross elastic.
If the XED coefficient is between -1 and +1 then the product is cross inelastic.

1.2.3 Price, income and cross elasticities of demand

Cross-elasticity of demand is determined by whether the product is a:
Substitute

- Substitutes will have a positive cross-elasticity of demand
- As the price of good y increases (positive) the demand for good x will increase (positive)
- Close substitutes will have a higher XED as consumer demand for good x will be more sensitive to a change in price of good y

Complement

- Complements will have a negative cross-elasticity of demand
- As the price of good y increases (positive) the demand for good x will decrease (negative)
- Close complements will have a higher XED as consumer demand for good x will be more sensitive to a change in price of good y

Has no relationship
- The change in the price of good x will have no impact on the demand for good y
- XED will be 0

1.2.3 Price, income and cross elasticities of demand

Elasticities of demand are important to firms.

Firms will attempt to change the cross-elasticity of their products by differentiating their products from the competition. This can be done through advertising and branding of the product so that consumers are less likely to switch to competitor's products. A firm with plenty of close substitutes will be less able to increase its prices.

Firms will produce a range of complements to accompany their core products. For example, Apple produce accessories, such as cases and docks, that consumers are likely to buy alongside their core products, such as the iPhone. A firm that sells a range of complements is likely to increase total revenue.

Elasticities of demand are important to government.

They will influence tax and subsidies. If demand for a good or service is **price inelastic** there will be little change if a **tax** is imposed. Government revenue will increase. A **subsidy** on these goods would see little change in demand but a large fall in price and consumers would benefit.

If demand for a good or service is **price elastic** there will be a significant decrease in demand if a tax is imposed and a large increase if there is a subsidy.

1.2.3 Price, income and cross elasticities of demand

1. Define the term "price elasticity of demand".
2. Would a firm prefer to have a more or less elastic PED coefficient? Justify your answer.
3. If a firm's product has a PED of -2.0 what will happen to demand if price rises by 5%?
4. If demand is perfectly inelastic what will happen to the volume of sales if price increased by 5%?
5. An increase in income leads to an increase in demand for steak and a decrease in demand for sausages. This suggests that:
   a. Sausages are price inelastic and steak is price elastic
   b. Sausages are an inferior good and steak is a normal good
   c. Sausages have a positive YED and steak has a negative YED
   d. The cross elasticity of demand between sausages and steak is 0
6. State **four** factors that help determine the income elasticity of demand.
7. If two products, A and B, are cross elastic what will happen to the demand for good B if the price of good A rises?

1.2.3 Price, income and cross elasticities of demand

8. If YED for a product is +2.0 what will happen to demand if incomes fall by 10%?

9. The table below shows the price of metals over a 2 year period

Metals	2013 ($ per tonne)	2014 ($ per tonne)
Aluminium	1900	1700
Copper	7000	7400
Lead	2400	2700
Zinc	2200	2600

Which **one** of the following is supported by the data?
   a. The decrease in the price of aluminium will lead to its increased supply
   b. The PED for copper is lower than that of the other metals
   c. Total revenue for lead producers will increase if demand for lead is price elastic
   d. Total revenue for zinc producers will increase if demand for lead is price inelastic

1. What is the relationship between substitute goods?

10. What is the relationship between complements?

Tick off each level reached as you progress through the sections

1.2.4 Supply

Supply: the amount of a good or service that producers are willing and able to sell at any given price at a set point in time.

The relationship between price and quantity supplied can be shown using a **supply curve.**

The supply curve shows the quantity supplied of a product, at any given price, over a period of time.

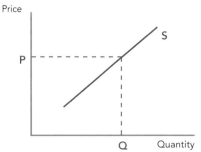

- As the price of a product rises quantity supplied will increase

- As the price of a product falls quantity supplied will decrease

1.2.4 Supply

A change in price is always shown by a **movement along** the supply curve.

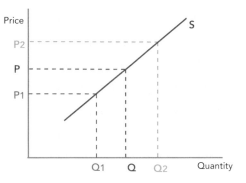

At price **P** the quantity supplied is **Q**.

If the price falls from **P** to **P1** the quantity supplied falls from **Q** to **Q1**.

If the price rises from **P** to **P2** the quantity supplied rises from **Q** to **Q2**.

1.2.4 Supply

There are a number of **determinants** or **factors** influencing the level of supply. The quantity supplied of a good or service is said to be a function of all of these factors. This can be shown mathematically:

- qs = f (p, production costs, technology, p of other goods/services, G policy, all other factors)
  - *qs = quantity supplied*
  - *f = is a function of*
  - *p = price*
  - *g = government*

The price of the good (p)
At higher prices firms are more likely to cover their costs allowing firms to make a profit. Firms are unlikely to produce if they are making a loss, particularly in the long-term. Therefore higher prices provide an incentive for firms to produce more of that product.

1.2.4 Supply

The impact of changing costs of production
Costs of production are created by the price of factor inputs i.e. the factors of production. If the cost of producing a good or service increases it will become more expensive to supply the product. This will lead to some firms reducing output.

The price of factor inputs can also be reduced making it cheaper to supply a product. If this happens there will be an increase in supply. Improvements in technology or labour productivity can help to reduce costs of production.

Technological progress
Technological progress has meant that firms can produce in a more efficient and cost effective manner. Improved large scale machinery allows them to spread fixed costs over greater output making the cost per unit produced cheaper. Therefore as technology improves firms find it profitable to supply more products.

1.2.4 Supply

Prices of other goods and services
A firm can use its factors of production to produce a range of products. If the price of good A increases this might make it more profitable to switch from good B in order to supply good A. New firms will enter markets with rising prices as there is a greater incentive to make profits.

Government policy e.g. taxes and subsidies
Indirect taxes make it more expensive to produce a product therefore the quantity supplied of that product will decrease. Subsidies will make it cheaper to produce a product therefore the quantity supplied of that product will increase.

Other factors e.g. expectations
A variety of other factors such as:

- expectations of future events

- the degree of competition in the market

- the power of firms within a market

1.2.4 Supply

If the change in supply is caused by any factor other than price then the supply curve **shifts.**

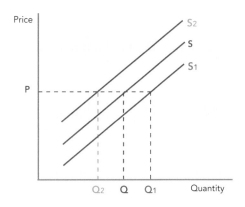

At price **P** the quantity supplied is **Q**.

If a change in a variable other than price causes an **increase** in supply the supply curve shifts **right** from **S** to **S1** and quantity supplied increases from **Q** to **Q1**.

If a change in a variable other than price causes a **decrease** in supply the supply curve shifts **left** from **S** to **S2** and quantity supplied decreases from **Q** to **Q2**.

1.2.4 Supply

1. Define the term "supply".

2. How might an indirect tax levied on a good impact on its supply?

3. If labour productivity were to increase what is the most likely impact on supply?

4. What is the relationship between quantity supplied and the price for a normal good?

5. Describe what happens to the supply curve if there is a change in price.

6. Describe what happens to the supply curve if there is a change in any factor other than price.

7. List **four** factors that influence the supply of a good or service.

8. Draw and correctly label a shift in the supply curve due to the impact of technological progress.

9. Draw and correctly label a shift in the supply curve due to the impact of poor weather conditions on a farming business.

1.2.4 Supply

10. The upward slope of the supply curve is due to which **one** of the following?

    a. The price of other goods

    b. Competition in the market

    c. The profit incentive at higher prices

    d. The PES of the product

11. Correctly label the following graph showing shifts in the supply curve.

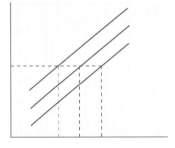

Tick off each level reached as you progress through the sections

1.2.5 Elasticity of supply

Price elasticity of supply (PES): measures the responsiveness of supply to a change in price.

Calculated using the formula:
$$\frac{\text{Percentage change in quantity supplied}}{\text{Percentage change in price}}$$

Or:
$$\frac{\% \Delta \text{ qs}}{\% \Delta \text{ p}}$$

> For example:
> The price of a good increases by 10%. This leads to a 7% increase in quantity supplied.
> +7%/+10% = +0.7 PES = +0.7

Price elastic: a change in price will lead to a more than proportional change in supply.

Price inelastic: a change in price will lead to a less than proportional change in supply.

If the PES coefficient is greater than 1 e.g. +1.5 then the product is price elastic.

If the PES coefficient is less than 1 e.g. +0.8 then the product is price inelastic.

Firms will try to increase their PES. A more elastic PES coefficient suggests that the firm is more flexible in changing the supply of its products, thereby making it more competitive.

1.2.4 Price Elasticity of Supply

Price elastic supply
A price elastic product will have a PES coefficient between 1 and infinity (∞). If price was to change the quantity supplied would change by a greater amount. Firms find it easy to increase supply or the incentive to increase supply has become greater.

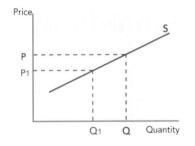

- an increase in P will lead to an increase in S greater than the increase in P

- a decrease in P will lead to a decrease in S greater than the decrease in P

The flatter the gradient of the supply curve the greater the level of elasticity.

A **perfectly elastic** product will have a PES coefficient of ∞. If price was to stay the same or increase the quantity supplied would be infinite. If price was to decrease the quantity supplied would fall to zero. This is shown by a horizontal supply curve.

1.2.5 Elasticity of supply

Price elastic supply
A price elastic product will have a PES coefficient between 1 and infinity (∞). If price was to change the quantity supplied would change by a greater amount. Firms find it easy to increase supply or the incentive to increase supply has become greater.

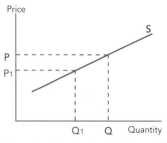

- an increase in P will lead to an increase in S greater than the increase in P

- a decrease in P will lead to a decrease in S greater than the decrease in P

The flatter the gradient of the supply curve the greater the level of elasticity.

A **perfectly elastic** product will have a PES coefficient of ∞. If price was to stay the same or increase the quantity supplied would be infinite. If price was to decrease the quantity supplied would fall to zero. This is shown by a horizontal supply curve.

1.2.5 Elasticity of supply

Price inelastic supply
A price inelastic product will have a PES coefficient between 0 and 1. If price was to change the quantity supplied would change by a lesser amount. This may be because of difficulties in increasing supply or that the incentive to increase supply is not great enough for some firms.

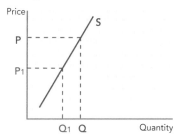

- an increase in P will lead to an increase in S less than the increase in P

- a decrease in P will lead to a decrease in S less than the decrease in P

The steeper the gradient of the supply curve the greater the level of inelasticity.

A **perfectly inelastic** product will have a PES coefficient of 0. If price was to change the quantity supplied would not be affected. In theory, the firm would supply the same amount at any given price. This is shown by a vertical supply curve.

1.2.5 Elasticity of supply

Price elasticity of supply is determined by:

Price
- Increases in price act as an incentive for firms to increase supply
- At higher price levels a firm is more profitable as the contribution per unit (selling price – variable cost) is higher

Substitutes
- The number and closeness of available substitutes
- If it is easy for a firm to increase production of its products e.g. from tables to chairs then PES is likely to be very price elastic. The easier it is to switch production the higher the PES

Time
- In the **short run** products are likely to be more price inelastic as producers find it difficult to change production
- In the **long run** products are likely to be more price elastic as producers adjust to changing market conditions by buying more machinery, building new factories etc.

1.2.5 Elasticity of supply

1. Define the term "price elasticity of supply".

2. Would a firm prefer to have a more or less elastic PES coefficient? Justify your answer.

3. PES for most goods and services has a figure that is:
   a. 0
   b. Between 0 and -1
   c. Positive
   d. Negative

4. If the PES coefficient and the change in price are given, what formula should be used to calculate the change in quantity supplied?

5. If the PES coefficient and the change in quantity supplied are given, what formula should be used to calculate the change in price?

6. What is the PES coefficient for a perfectly elastic product?

7. What is the PES coefficient for a perfectly inelastic product?

Test Yourself

1.2.5 Elasticity of supply

8. Which **one** of the following is a major determinant of the elasticity of supply of a good?

    a. The price of the good
    b. The YED of the good
    c. Spare capacity available
    d. The PED of the good

9. What is the shape of an elastic supply curve?

10. What is the shape of an inelastic supply curve?

11. What happens to the PES of housing over the long run?

12. Calculate the PES for the products in the table if price were to change from £50 to £75 for each product.

	Good A	Good B	Good C	Good D
£50	50	100	20	40
£75	100	110	25	40

Tick off each level reached as you progress through the sections

1.2.6 Price determination

Market equilibrium: point at which demand is equal to supply.

Equilibrium price: the price at which demand equals supply and therefore all products will be sold. This is known as the **market clearing price:**

- All buyers can get the exact amount that they want to buy at this price and all sellers provide exactly the amount that they want to sell at this price

- Therefore there is nothing left over i.e. the market has cleared

Market equilibrium can be shown graphically as the point where the demand curve crosses the supply curve.

At a price of P quantity demanded (qd) is equal to quantity supplied (qs).
At this price all products that have been offered for sale by suppliers have been bought by buyers i.e. all supply has had an equal demand.

1.2.6 Price determination

Disequilibrium occurs when there is an imbalance in the quantity demanded and quantity supplied of a product i.e. there is excess demand or excess supply.

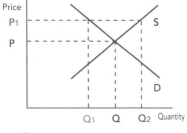

If price were to rise from **P** to **P1** there would be **excess supply**. Buyers would demand less (Q1) at the higher price but firms would wish to supply more (Q2) at this price. This would lead to a situation of too much supply (Q2 – Q1) in the market. To solve this problem firms would need to lower price to get rid of excess products.

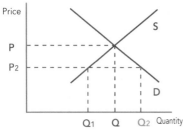

If price were to fall from **P** to **P2** there would be **excess demand**. Buyers would demand more (Q2) at the lower price but firms would wish to supply less (Q1) at this price. This would lead to a situation of too much demand (Q2 – Q1) in the market. To improve profitability firms could raise price, thus reducing the excess demand.

1.2.6 Price determination

Market forces are always pushing prices towards market equilibrium i.e. the price at which demand equals supply and there are no products left over in the market.

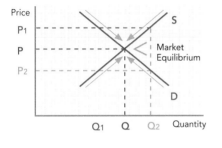

- Too much supply leads to lower prices
- Too much demand leads to higher prices

A change in price will lead to a movement along the supply or demand curve. Whereas a change in any other factor will lead to a shift in the demand or supply curve. Any changes in demand or supply will lead to a new equilibrium price.

1.2.6 Price determination

A shift in demand will lead to a movement along the supply curve.

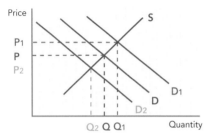

An increase in demand will see the demand curve shift **upwards** and **towards the right** from D to D1. This will cause price to rise to P1 and quantity demanded to Q1. At this point there is a new market equilibrium of P1 Q1.

A decrease in demand will see the demand curve shift **downwards** and **towards the left** from D to D2. This will cause price to fall to P2 and quantity demanded to Q2. At this point there is a new market equilibrium of P2 Q2.

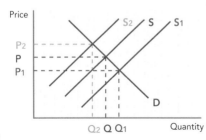

A shift in supply will lead to a movement along the demand curve. An increase in supply will see the supply curve shift **downwards** and **towards the right** from S to S1. This will cause price to fall to P1 and quantity supplied to rise to Q1. At this point there is a new market equilibrium of P1 Q1.

A decrease in supply will see the supply curve shift **upwards** and **towards the left** from S to S2. This will cause price to rise to P2 and quantity supplied to fall to Q2. At this point there is a new market equilibrium of P2 Q2.

1.2.6 Price determination

Changes in demand and supply cause equilibrium price and quantity to change in real-world situations.

Commodity markets:

A commodity market is one where buyers and sellers come together to exchange homogeneous products. They do not exhibit product differentiation and are therefore likely to be unbranded. This means that the price of the product is determined by the market as a whole i.e. aggregate demand in the market. This can be compared to other markets such as retailing where some form of branding differentiates the product e.g. Nike sportswear and therefore impacts on price.

Hard commodities are those that are extracted from the ground and include metals such as gold, silver, copper and platinum. These tend to be non-renewable resources. **Soft commodities** are those that can be grown such as coffee, tea, wheat and sugar. The quality of commodities can differ and can therefore be categorised into subsectors e.g. 24 carat and 9 carat gold.

Commodities are subject to **speculation** by traders. If they believe that the price of gold is set to rise they might invest in the metal. This leads to a self-fulfilling prophesy. If the majority of commodity traders believe that the price of gold is set to rise they will buy the commodity. A rise in demand will shift the demand curve to the right, leading to an increase in its price.

1.2.6 Price determination

Commodities exhibit inelastic supply. Firstly, there is limited supply of non-renewable resources such as gold. Therefore, any increases in demand will lead to an exacerbated increase in price. Secondly, even if new sources were discovered, it takes time and money to extract e.g. opening new mines. New discoveries tend to be harder to extract as they are likely to be further underground or more difficult to access. At first it may be uneconomical to mine these. As price increases costs are covered and the extraction becomes profitable.

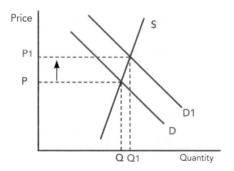

1.2.6 Price determination

Agricultural products are a type of soft commodity as they are grown. These products are characterised by variable shifts in the supply curve as they are significantly affected by changes in weather and climate. For example, flooding, drought and disease can have a dramatic impact on the supply of agricultural products.

Supply tends to be inelastic for specific crops in the short term as there is a time lag between deciding what crops to grow and when they are available to harvest. This is exacerbated when there is an adverse climate leading to spikes in the price of some foodstuffs. When weather conditions are good there is the likelihood of a bumper crop. A glut of agricultural products will see excess supply and price will be forced down. This has led to serious cash flow problems for farmers, some of whom can be forced out of business through either a poor harvest and therefore low income or a bumper crop forcing prices down and leading to low sales revenue. As a result, governments have intervened in the market, using **buffer stocks** to reduce fluctuations in price and output.

1.2.6 Price determination

As both the global population and incomes have risen demand for agricultural products has increased. There has been a long term shift to the right of the demand curve. However, intensive farming and developments in technology have led to a long term shift to the right of the supply curve. Over time the supply curve becomes more elastic as farmers can plan output. In recent years, rapid population growth and increases in incomes in emerging markets has helped to see demand for agricultural products outstrip supply. This has led to shortages and increases in price.

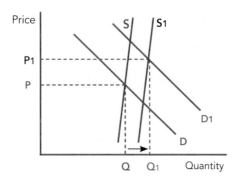

1.2.6 Price determination

Health care:

Health care is seen as a **merit good**. Therefore, its consumption benefits society. However, it is also expensive. In the UK the Government has invested heavily into health care since the end of the Second World War in 1945, particularly through the National Health Service (NHS). The NHS is estimated to be the biggest employer in Europe with over 1.5m workers. It is the second most expensive item in the Government's budget, after payments for social benefits such as jobseeker's allowance. Therefore, in the UK, the supply curve is further to the right than in many other countries. For example, in the US, patients have traditionally insured themselves for health care.

Despite heavy investment it is recognised that there are problems in the NHS e.g. waiting lists. The demand for health care reflects modern life. Obesity, smoking, alcoholism and increased life spans has led to increasing demand. This has seen increases in the supply of private health care, such as BUPA. As this is often a fringe benefit for professional workers, and is therefore paid for by the business, there is a high demand.

1.2.6 Price determination

At the same time those with high incomes see the provision of good health care as essential for both themselves and their families. These workers are both willing and able to pay for health care, leading to a price inelastic demand. Private businesses are therefore confident that there will be a demand for their services so they are willing to spend on capital investment to increase supply.

As demand for health care outstrips supply there will be a rationing mechanism. In the NHS this is provided for through waiting lists. For private health care additional costs for some services have to be paid. Higher prices reduce demand.

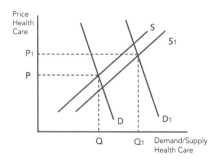

1.2.6 Price determination

Housing:

The demand for housing is a complex matter. Housing is seen as a basic need, rather than a luxury. All people require somewhere to live. However, for some, housing is seen as a form of investment. Over time, house prices tend to appreciate in the UK. As house prices rise the value of people's wealth increases. This can be utilised as people release equity from their houses e.g. a bank loan against the increased value of the house. This can lead to knock on effects in the economy as people increase spending through borrowing. Unlike a normal good, an increase in house prices leads to increased demand. This is due to expectations of rising prices in the future. It is recognised that house prices today will be lower than house prices in a year's time. Therefore, increases in price have led to increased demand. In addition, income and population growth has led to increased demand.

The level of demand is further complicated by the rental market. Housing is seen as an investment good, leading to a stream of income in the future for landlords. This means that demand is exacerbated as investors see **income growth** through rent and **capital growth** through the appreciation of the house price.

1.2.6 Price determination

The **supply of housing** is also a complex matter. Government restrictions on building in certain areas such as green belt land reduce the space available to build on. The Government has reduced the number of council houses available for those on lower incomes to rent. Therefore, demand for new houses and rental accommodation has increased people moving from council housing into the private sector. The Government do provide council housing, and housing associations provide social housing, at below market price for rental accommodation. Private companies have built new houses and the style of houses e.g. an increase in flats has led to a greater concentration of households. In the short run the housing supply is highly inelastic due to planning restrictions and build time. In the long run supply can increase but a lack of political conviction to reduce restrictions on new building means that demand has continued to outstrip supply.

House prices increase over both the short and long run. Periodically there might be a dramatic fall in prices as factors such as recession mean that people cannot afford to repay their mortgages. As houses are repossessed there is greater availability of housing. There is less confidence and demand falls. Excess supply leads to lower prices. New buyers might wait for prices to fall further. There is then a downward spiral in prices until the economy starts to recover.

1.2.6 Price determination

1. Define the term "equilibrium price".
2. Define the term "market equilibrium".
3. Draw and correctly label a diagram showing market equilibrium.
4. At the equilibrium price in a market how many units of a good are left over?
5. Define the term "disequilibrium".
6. Define the term "excess demand".
7. Draw and correctly label a diagram showing excess demand.
8. Define the term "excess supply".
9. Draw and correctly label a diagram showing excess supply.
10. Define the term "market forces".
11. Using an appropriate diagram, explain how market forces push price towards equilibrium.
12. Draw and correctly label a diagram showing what will happen if there is an increase in demand for a good.

1.2.6 Price determination

13. Plot a demand and supply curve for the following data. What is the equilibrium price?

Price (£)	Quantity demanded (000s)	Quantity supplied (000s)
10	6000	2000
20	4000	4000
30	2000	6000

14. With reference to the diagram above explain the relationship between demand and supply at a price of £10 and a price of £30.

15. Draw and correctly label a diagram showing what will happen if there is a decrease in the supply of a good.

16. If the size of the UK population continues to grow explain, with the use of a diagram, what will happen to price and output for a good or service in the market.

17. If new technology reduces the unit costs of producing a good explain, with the use of a diagram, what will happen to price and output for a good or service in the market.

Tick off each level reached as you progress through the sections

1.2.7 Price mechanism

In a market economy **prices** perform the function of allocating resources and co-ordinating the decisions of buyers and sellers. This is influenced by the following **functions of prices**:

The rationing function
Excess demand for a good or service will lead to a rise in its price. This is due to the scarcity of the product. The increase in price will consequently lead to a reduction in demand. The higher price restricts the number of buyers who are willing and able to buy the product. As the use of the product becomes restricted its availability is effectively rationed. There will therefore be a movement along the demand curve showing an increase in price and a decrease in quantity demanded.

The incentive function
Higher prices act as a motivator for producers to increase the supply of a good or service. This is due to greater contribution per unit i.e. the difference between selling price and variable cost. Ceteris paribus, as prices increase so do revenue and profit providing a greater incentive to supply the product. There will be a movement along the supply curve showing an increase in quantity supplied.

1.2.7 Price mechanism

The signalling function

An increase in price will give an indication to producers that they should increase supply and an indication to consumers that they should reduce demand. A decrease in price will give an indication to producers that they should decrease supply and an indication to consumers that they should increase demand. All of these signals will lead to shifts in the supply or demand curves.

Allocative efficiency occurs where consumer satisfaction is maximised in the production of goods and services. At this point quantity supplied will equal quantity demanded. Society is producing goods to match the needs of consumers. Allocative efficiency is difficult to identify as the economy needs to match consumer preferences to producer output. Markets do not always operate at the market clearing price due to:

- Excess supply (S>D)

- Excess demand (D>S)

Market forces do push prices towards equilibrium where quantity demanded will equal quantity supplied. Therefore, it is likely that competitive markets help in achieving allocative efficiency.

1.2.7 Price mechanism

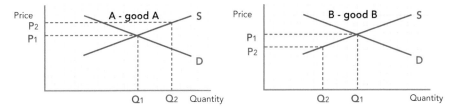

In diagram A suppose the market price for good A is P2. In diagram B the market price for good B is also P2. There is allocative inefficiency. By reallocating resources from the production of good A to good B allocative efficiency can be increased. This can be seen at Q1.

In diagram A the market price is P2. Consumers value the last unit produced at Q1 where price is P1. However, firms produce at Q2. Consumers are not willing to pay the higher price so price will fall and firms reduce supply. This might lead to a reallocation of firms' resources to another use e.g. from good A to good B. In diagram B suppose the market price is P2. Consumers value the last unit produced at Q1 where price is P1. However, firms produce at Q2. Consumers are willing to pay the higher price so price will rise to P2 and firms will increase supply. This might lead to a reallocation of firms' resources from another use e.g. from good A to good B.

Test Yourself

1.2.7 Price mechanism

1. Define the term "rationing function".

2. Define the term "signalling function".

3. Define the term "incentive function".

4. Define the term "allocative efficiency".

5. Define the term "allocative inefficiency".

6. With the use of an appropriate example and diagrams explain how markets might reallocate resources between different goods.

Tick off each level reached as you progress through the sections

1.2.8 Consumer and producer surplus

Consumer surplus is the difference between the price a consumer is willing to pay for a product and the price that they actually pay. For example, a consumer might be willing to pay £400 for a bike that retails at £600. The surplus value that the consumer has gained is therefore £200.

Consumer surplus can be shown diagrammatically:

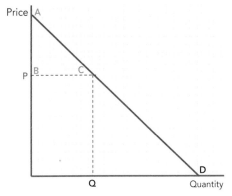

The area ABC shows the consumer surplus that is received by those consumers who would have been willing to pay more than price P.

The triangle shows the difference between quantity demanded at a range of given prices (portion A – C of the demand curve) and the price (P) that consumers actually pay (portion B – C). The area ABC is known as consumer surplus.

1.2.8 Consumer and producer surplus

The impact on consumer surplus of changes in price.

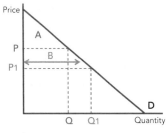

At price P and quantity Q consumer surplus is shown by A.
If a firm reduces price to P1 then quantity demanded will increase to Q1. Consumer surplus will increase by area B. Total consumer surplus will be the area A+B.

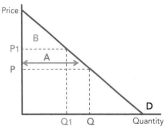

At price P and quantity Q consumer surplus is shown by A+B.
If a firm increases price to P1 then quantity demanded will decrease to Q1. Consumer surplus will decrease by area A. Total consumer surplus will be the area B.

1.2.8 Consumer and producer surplus

Producer surplus is the difference between the price a producer is willing to supply a product at and the price actually received for the product. For example, a producer might be willing to supply a bike for £300 but actually sells it for £800. The surplus value that the producer has gained is therefore £500.
This can be shown diagrammatically:

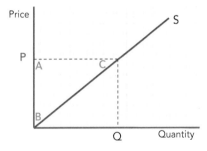

The area ABC shows the producer surplus that is received by firms.

The triangle shows the difference between the price at which firms are willing to supply at a range of given prices (portion B – C of the supply curve) and the price (P) that producers actually receive (portion A – C). The area ABC is known as producer surplus.

1.2.8 Consumer and producer surplus

The impact on producer surplus of changes in price.

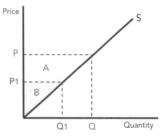

At price **P** and quantity **Q** producer surplus is shown by area **A+B**.

If price were to fall to **P1** then quantity supplied will decrease to **Q1**.
Producer surplus will decrease by area **A**.
Total producer surplus will be the area **B**.

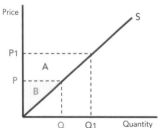

At price **P** and quantity **Q** producer surplus is shown by **B**.

If price were to increase to **P1** then quantity supplied will increase to **Q1**. Producer surplus will increase by area **A**. Total producer surplus will be the area **A+B**.

1.2.8 Consumer and producer surplus

Consumer and producer surplus can be shown on the same diagram.

Blue represents consumer surplus and green producer surplus.

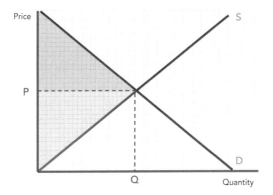

1.2.8 Consumer and producer surplus

How changes in demand and supply impact on consumer and producer surplus

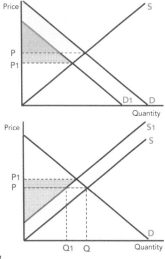

A reduction in demand will lead to a fall in consumer surplus e.g. a shift in the demand curve to the left from **D** to **D1**, and vice versa.

This will lead consumer surplus falling from the larger green/yellow shaded area to the smaller green/blue shaded area.

A reduction in supply will lead to a fall in producer surplus e.g. a shift in the supply curve to the left from **S** to **S1**, and vice versa.

This will lead to producer surplus falling from the larger green/yellow shaded area to the smaller green/blue shaded area.

1.2.8 Consumer and producer surplus

1. Define the term "consumer surplus".

2. Define the term "producer surplus".

3. With the use of an appropriate diagram, illustrate the concept of consumer surplus.

4. With the use of an appropriate diagram, illustrate the concept of producer surplus.

5. With the use of an appropriate diagram, illustrate the impact on consumer surplus of changes in price.

6. With the use of an appropriate diagram, illustrate the impact on producer surplus of changes in price.

7. With the use of an appropriate diagram, illustrate the impact on consumer surplus of changes in demand and supply.

8. With the use of an appropriate diagram, illustrate the impact on producer surplus of changes in demand and supply.

Tick off each level reached as you progress through the sections

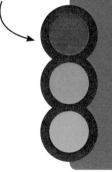

1.2.9 Indirect taxes and subsidies

Indirect taxation
Taxation is the medium through which governments finance their spending and control the economy. An indirect tax is a tax on a good or a service. A direct tax is a tax on an individual or an organisation. The incidence, or burden, of tax is the amount that the consumer or producer will pay for the tax.

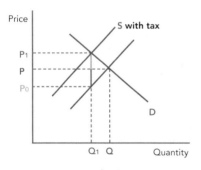

The imposition of an indirect tax will lead to an increase in the cost of supply for a firm. This will lead to a shift in the supply curve up and to the left. Quantity supplied will decrease by Q-Q1. Price will increase from P to P1. The incidence of the tax paid for by the producer is shown by the blue line, equivalent to P-P0. The incidence of the tax paid for by the consumer is shown by the green line, equivalent to P1-P. The revenue raised for the government by the tax is the distance from P0 to P1 multiplied by Q1.

1.2.9 Indirect taxes and subsidies

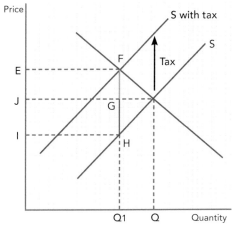

1. Incidence of tax on consumers = FG
2. Incidence of tax on producers = GH
3. Tax paid by consumers = EFGJ
4. Tax paid by producers = GHIJ
5. Government revenue from tax = EFHI

1.2.9 Indirect taxes and subsidies

Specific and ad valorem taxes

A **specific tax** is a set amount per unit, for example, a tax of £4.57 per packet of 20 cigarettes in 2018.

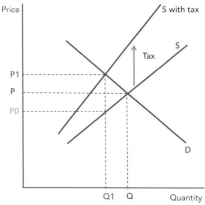

An **ad valorem tax** is a percentage of the price of the good or service. Therefore, the more expensive the product the greater the tax levied on it. For example, there is a 16.5% ad valorem tax on the retail price on a packet of 20 cigarettes, in 2018.

An ad valorem tax will shift the supply curve upwards whilst also tilting it. As price increases the tax increases.

1.2.9 Indirect taxes and subsidies

The impact and incidence of indirect taxes

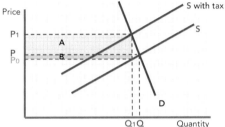

If demand is price inelastic the incidence of the tax will be greater for the consumer. This can be seen with area A greater than area B.

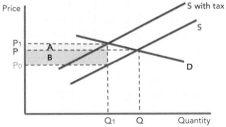

If demand is price elastic the incidence of the tax will be greater for the producer. This can be seen with area B greater than area A.

1.2.9 Indirect taxes and subsidies

Subsidy
A subsidy is a financial incentive to produce or consume a given product.

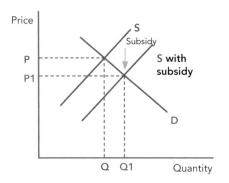

The imposition of a subsidy will lead to a decrease in the cost of supply for a firm. This will lead to a shift in the supply curve down and to the right. Quantity supplied will increase by Q-Q1. Price will decrease from P to P1.

The subsidy will be shared between the consumer and the producer.

1.2.9 Indirect taxes and subsidies

Consumer and producer subsidy
A subsidy is a financial incentive to produce or consume a given product.

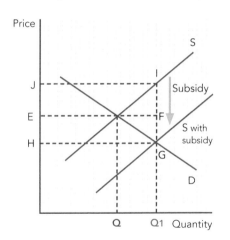

The imposition of a subsidy will lead to a decrease in the cost of supply for a firm. This will lead to a shift in the supply curve down and to the right. Quantity supplied will increase by Q-Q1. Price will decrease from P to P1.

The subsidy will be shared between the consumer and the producer.

1. Gain to consumers = EFGH
2. Gain to producers = EFIJ
3. Incidence of subsidy on government = IG
4. Government expenditure on subsidy = GHJI

1.2.9 Indirect taxes and subsidies

1. Define the term "indirect tax".

2. Define the term "incidence of tax".

3. Define the term "subsidy".

4. With the use of an appropriate diagram, illustrate the impact on a firm of the imposition of an indirect tax.

5. On your diagram show the following:

   a. Incidence of the tax on the producer

   b. Incidence of the tax on the consumer

   c. Tax paid by consumers

   d. Tax paid by producers

   e. Government revenue from tax

1.2.9 Indirect taxes and subsidies

6. With the use of an appropriate diagram, illustrate the impact on a firm of a subsidy.

7. On your diagram show the following:

    a. Gain to consumers

    b. Gain to producers

    c. Incidence of subsidy on government

    d. Government expenditure on subsidy

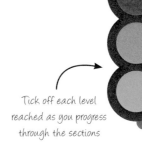

Tick off each level reached as you progress through the sections

1.2.10 Alternative views of consumer behaviour

Behavioural economics looks at the psychological reasons behind why people make decisions.

Bounded rationality suggests that when people make decisions they are limited by:
- The information available to them
- Their intellectual limitations
- The time available to make decisions

Therefore, we can influence people's decision-making. A number of factors influence this:

Social norms are the rules of behaviour that are considered acceptable within a social group. People who don't follow social norms are often not accepted within the group. Therefore, individuals will attempt to 'fit in' with the crowd by following social norms. This might even mean that consumption of a good or service leads to marginal disutility.

Nudge theory is an attempt to manipulate social norms through positive reinforcement in a non-coercive manner.

1.2.10 Alternative views of consumer behaviour

Habitual behaviour occurs when people follow the same routines, repeating actions on a regular basis. Some habitual behaviour can be healthy e.g. exercise but some can be bad for the individual e.g. smoking.

Maintaining the status quo means that economic agents might suffer from **loss aversion**, making decisions based on avoiding loss rather than achieving gain. However, people quickly **adapt** to new routines and will find it difficult to revert back to old routines e.g. if I buy a bigger car I will find it difficult to revert back to a smaller car.

Often, consumers have a weakness in day to day **computation**, the ability to make correct decisions based on the information available to them. Individuals make judgements based on mental short cuts when uncertainty exists and when it is too difficult to compute the available information.

1.2.10 Alternative views of consumer behaviour

A **heuristic** is a simple rule that individuals use to make a judgement when undertaking decision-making. They normally focus on one aspect of a problem rather than looking at all the information available. Therefore, decision-making is flawed.

Tversky and Kahneman named three **heuristics** that can lead to irrational behaviour by individuals:

- **Availability** – making judgements based on, particularly vivid, events we can remember rather than the information at hand e.g. we might fear flying due to excessive media coverage but the likelihood of a plane crash is negligible

- **Representativeness** – categorising based on past information rather than on the information at hand e.g. a gambler might make a bet because they believe that they are in a run of good luck

- **Anchoring and adjustment** – using an arbitrary starting number to estimate a different number. The starting number is the anchor and we tend to adjust an answer to be close to the anchor e.g. Is the population of Brazil higher or lower than 100m? What is the population of Brazil? Often people will give a figure close to 100m

1.2.10 Alternative views of consumer behaviour

1. Explain three reasons why individuals are limited in their decision-making skills.

2. Define the term "habitual behaviour".

3. Define the term "loss aversion".

4. Define the term "consumer weakness at computation".

5. Define the term "heuristic".

6. State three heuristics that can lead to irrational behaviour by individuals.

Tick off each level reached as you progress through the sections

1.3.1 Types of market failure

Market failure occurs when the allocation of goods and services are inefficient. This means that some consumers can be made better off without making others worse off. The market is unable to efficiently allocate scarce resources to meet the needs of society. In practice, there will always be market failure, also known as **allocative inefficiency**. It is the role of government to try to eliminate market failure. They do this by intervening in markets (**government intervention**).

Complete market failure occurs when there is no market whatsoever i.e. a missing market. Goods and services will not be supplied to the market as firms will not receive revenue for supplying the product e.g. street lighting.

Partial market failure occurs when a market exists but there is a misallocation of resources. Goods and services will be supplied but in the wrong amounts e.g. merit and demerit goods.

1.3.1 Types of market failure

The market creates the mechanism for allocating scarce resources. However, markets are often inefficient in doing this job i.e. there is a **misallocation of resources**.

This may be because of:

Externalities

- The costs and benefits to a third party created by economic agents when undertaking their activities. These costs and benefits can be either negative or positive

Under-provision of public goods

- When firms do not provide goods and services because they find it difficult to charge for the product

Information gaps

- When consumers have asymmetric information, where some parties in a transaction have more information regarding the product than others

1.3.2 Externalities

Externalities: the costs and benefits to a third party created by economic agents when undertaking their activities.

These costs and benefits can be **negative** or **positive.**

Negative externalities: those costs to a third party that are not included in the price of the economic activity.

Negative externalities arise as a result of the divergence between **private costs** and **social costs**. Private costs are those costs of consuming or producing goods or services that have to be paid for by third parties e.g. the individual or a firm. Social costs are those costs of consuming or producing goods or services that are paid for by society, including private costs.

Negative externalities exist when social costs are greater than private costs. These additional costs to consumption or production are not paid for by the economic unit such as the individual or the firm. Examples of negative externalities include:

- Pollution e.g. air and water
- Road congestion
- Environmental damag

1.3.2 Externalities

Positive externalities: those benefits to a third party that are not included in the price of the economic activity.

Positive externalities arise as a result of the divergence between **private benefits** and **social benefits.** Private benefits are those benefits of consuming or producing goods or services that are received by an economic unit e.g. the individual or a firm. These are paid for. Social benefits are those benefits of consuming or producing goods or services that are received by society. Social benefits include private benefits but the difference between private and social benefits are unpaid for, creating the free rider problem.

Positive externalities exist when social benefits are greater than private benefits. These additional social benefits to consumption or production are not paid for by the economic unit such as the individual or the firm. Examples of positive externalities include:

- Educated society
- Medical breakthroughs
- Attractive environment

1.3.2 Externalities

Marginal analysis can be used to enhance our understanding of externalities. This looks at the benefit or cost we receive from consuming or producing one more unit:

- **Marginal benefit** is the benefit to a consumer of consuming one more unit of a good or service
- **Marginal cost** is the cost to a producer of producing one more unit of a good or service

Demand is the same as marginal private benefit

Marginal private benefit (MPB) is the additional amount of satisfaction that a

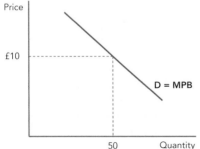

consumer gains from an additional unit of a good or service. MPB can be represented by the demand curve. The vertical distance at each quantity e.g. 50 units shows the amount consumers are willing to pay for that unit e.g. £10. This reflects the benefit derived from each unit. This can be recognised in the lower price that consumers are willing to pay for an additional unit as satisfaction decreases as we consume more. Therefore **D = MPB**.

1.3.2 Externalities

Allocative efficiency occurs where Price = Marginal Cost

If the price of producing a product is above the marginal cost of producing it then firms should increase output. As the price is above the cost of production the firm will increase output and make additional profit. Firms will allocate more resources into producing the product until price is equal to marginal cost (P = MC). At this point the firm is maximising profits. If MC was greater than P the firm would be making a loss on producing each additional unit.

Supply is the same as marginal private cost

Marginal private cost (MPC) is the cost to a producer of producing an additional unit. MPC can be represented by the supply curve. If the price of an additional unit pays for the cost of producing the extra unit then a firm will supply it. The supply curve reflects this as higher prices will lead to more being supplied as firms cover their costs for producing the additional unit. As price increases we will see an increase in supply as it is more likely that producers will cover their costs.

1.3.2 Externalities

As cost increases a producer can only make a profit from an additional unit if price is higher or equal to the cost of producing that additional unit. The point at which a firm stops supplying is when the additional cost is higher than the price received for producing that additional unit.

The marginal private cost curve therefore shows the relationship between costs, price and the quantity supplied of that product.

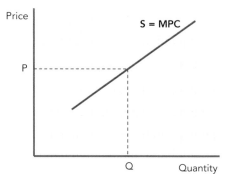

1.3.2 Externalities

Marginal social benefits (MSB) are those benefits of consuming or producing an additional unit of goods or services that are received by society. This will include marginal private benefits.
MSB = MPB + MEB.

Marginal social costs (MSC) are those costs of consuming or producing an additional unit of goods or services that are paid for by society. This will include marginal private costs.
MSC = MPC + MEC.

We can use **marginal social benefits** (MSB) and **marginal social costs** (MSC) to enhance our understanding of externalities. MSB includes MPB but also the additional benefits to society of consuming or producing one extra unit. We call these **marginal external benefits (MEB)**.

MSC includes MPC but also the additional costs to society of consuming or producing one extra unit. We call these **marginal external costs (MEC)**.

1.3.2 Externalities

The **market optimum position** occurs where MPB = MPC.
In a market economy the economic unit only considers the private costs or benefits of its activities. Consumers and producers will operate in a market where: MPB = MPC. This will lead to the maximisation of private benefit.

If MPB < MPC then consumers can achieve additional benefit from consuming more goods and services. If MPB > MPC then producers can achieve additional profits by increasing supply.
When MPB = MPC the market is in equilibrium.

Both negative and positive externalities lead to market failure because the private consumer or producer is not paying for, or receiving, the full cost or benefit of the economic activity.

1.3.2 Externalities

Negative production externalities: when the activities of producers lead to costs to a third party that are not included in the price of the economic activity.

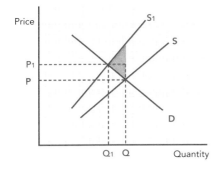

A firm's optimal level of output is Q. Society's optimal level of output is Q1. Therefore, the firm is **overproducing** by Q – Q1. Price is too low and output too high which has resulted in **allocative inefficiency**.

Supply curve S takes into account the cost to the firm of producing the product i.e. the private cost. If the cost to society is included the supply curve would shift up and to the left to S1. The costs to society of a negative externality will be greater than the costs to the producer.

If social costs were included i.e. the full costs then we would operate where S1 = D at P1Q1. The cost to society, or **welfare loss,** can be seen by the grey shaded area. This measures the difference between the social cost and private cost at output levels between Q and Q1.

1.3.2 Externalities

Positive production externalities: when the activities of producers lead to benefits for a third party that are not included in the price of the economic activity.

Welfare gain: a situation where the social cost is lower than the private cost and society gains as it does not have to pay for the difference.

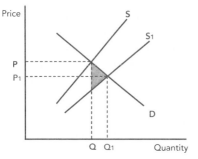

A firm's optimal level of output is Q. Society's optimal level of output is Q_1. Therefore, the firm is **under producing** by $Q - Q_1$. Price is too high and output too low which has resulted in **allocative inefficiency**.

Supply curve S_1 is down and to the right of S as the costs to society of a positive externality will be less than the costs to the producer.

If social costs were included i.e. the full costs then we would operate where $S_1 = D$ at P_1Q_1.

The benefit to society, or **welfare gain**, can be seen by the grey shaded area. This measures the difference between the social cost and private cost at output levels between Q and Q_1.

1.3.2 Externalities

Negative consumption externalities: when the activities of consumers lead to a loss of benefit to a third party that are not included in the price of the economic activity.

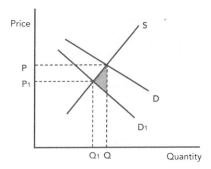

The consumer's optimal level of output is Q. Society's optimal level of output is Q_1. Therefore, the consumer is **over consuming** by $Q - Q_1$.

The consumer gains the benefit of consuming a good or service on the demand curve D. Social benefit is below and to the left of private benefit as the benefits to society of a negative externality will be lower than the benefits to the individual consumer. A consumer will maximise its private benefit by consuming where $S = D$ at PQ.

If social benefits were included we would operate where $S = D_1$ at P_1Q_1. The loss of benefit to society, or **welfare loss**, can be seen by the grey shaded area. This measures the difference between social benefit and private benefit at output levels between Q and Q_1.

1.3.2 Externalities

Positive consumption externalities: when the activities of consumers lead to benefits to a third party that are not included in the price of the economic activity.

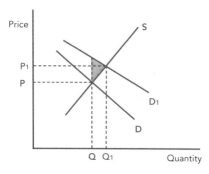

The consumer's optimal level of output is Q. Society's optimal level of output is Q_1. Therefore, society is benefiting over and above the individual consumer by $Q - Q_1$. The consumer is **under consuming**.

The consumer gains the benefit of consuming a good or service on the demand curve D. Social benefit is above and to the right of private benefit D_1 as the benefits to society of a positive externality will be greater than the benefits to the individual consumer. A consumer will maximise its private benefit by consuming where $S = D$ at PQ.

If social benefits were included we would operate where $S = D_1$ at P_1Q_1. The benefit to society, or **welfare gain**, can be seen by the grey shaded area. This measures the difference between social benefit and private benefit at output levels between Q and Q_1.

1.3.2 Externalities

The **social optimum position** occurs where MSB = MSC.

In order to eliminate externalities as a market failure the market needs to operate where MSB = MSC. As can be seen with our look at four types of externalities this is unlikely to happen. Economic units will look to operate where MPB = MPC whilst society will benefit where MSB = MSC. Neither producers nor consumers will take into account the needs of society.

Therefore, the divergence between private costs and benefits and social costs and benefits leads to government intervention.

This will occur in a variety of markets. Some of the most important include transport, health care and economic activity that impacts on the environment. These can be expensive, cause pollution and create negative externalities.

1.3.2 Externalities

1. Define the term "positive externalities".
2. Define the term "negative externalities".
3. Distinguish between "consumption externalities" and "production externalities".
4. Explain, with the aid of a diagram, a market within which private benefits are greater than social benefits.
5. Explain why society will benefit if the market displays the characteristics shown in the diagram below.

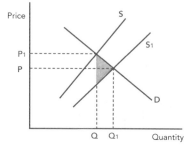

Test Yourself

1.3.2 Externalities

6. Explain, with the aid of a diagram, a situation in which the market has negative production externalities.

7. Explain, with the aid of a diagram, a situation in which the market has positive production externalities.

8. Explain, with the aid of a diagram, a situation in which the market has negative consumption externalities.

9. Explain, with the aid of a diagram, a situation in which the market has positive consumption externalities.

Tick off each level reached as you progress through the sections

1.3.3 Public goods

Public goods: one where its use by an individual does not stop others from using it whilst its consumption does not reduce the amount available for consumption by others.

Public goods are characterised as:

- **Non-rival goods** - the consumption of the good does not reduce the amount available for consumption by others

- **Non-excludable goods** - once provided it is impossible to stop other individuals from using them

Public goods can have positive or negative externalities. The army and street lighting are examples of public goods. With little incentive for firms to supply public goods the government is likely to intervene.

A **pure public good** is one where it is impossible to exclude someone from consuming it if they are unwilling to pay for its use e.g. the air that we breathe.

Market failure occurs due to the **free rider** problem. A **free rider** is someone who benefits from a good or service without paying for it.

1.3.3 Public goods

Private goods: one where its use by an individual stops others from using it whilst its consumption reduces the amount available for consumption by others.

Private goods are characterised as:

- **Rival goods** – the consumption of the good reduces the amount available for consumption by others
- **Excludable goods** - once provided it is possible to stop other individuals from using them

Private goods can have positive or negative externalities. Clothing and cars are examples of private goods. Firms can make a profit from providing private goods and services. There is therefore an incentive to produce them.

Some private goods take on some of the characteristics of public goods. These are called **quasi-public goods**. For example, consumers can be stopped from using a product that is normally free e.g. restricting access to a beach or to a public park. The word quasi means '*having a likeness to*'. A quasi-public good is a private good that is similar to a pure public good but there is an ability to stop non-paying consumers from using it.

1.3.3 Public goods

Test Yourself

1. Define the term "public goods".

2. Distinguish between the terms "non-rival" and "non-excludable goods".

3. Define the term "pure public good".

4. Distinguish between the terms "public" and "private" goods.

5. Distinguish between the terms "rival" and "excludable" goods.

6. Define the term "quasi-public good".

1.3.3 Public goods

7. A pure public good is one that

a. Is available to anyone at the market price if they can afford it

b. Is impossible to stop others consuming if they haven't paid for it

c. Is provided free of charge to all consumers by the government

d. Is a merit good that is provided free of charge to benefit society

8. Define the term "free rider".

9. Private goods are which one combination of the following?

a. Excludable and non-rival

b. Non-excludable and non-rival

c. Non-excludable and rival

d. Excludable and rival

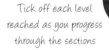

Tick off each level reached as you progress through the sections

1.3.4 Information gaps

Provision of information ensures that economic units can maximise decisions when consuming and producing goods and services. The government will provide information where the private sector fails to do so. It provides this information in a variety of areas e.g. the job market, dangerous products such as cigarettes or economic data to help firms plan for the future. The greater the information available to consumers the more likely they are to buy goods and services with confidence.

Information failure is a type of market failure where consumers or producers do not have **symmetric information** and therefore have **asymmetric information**. Without having full information about a product it is difficult for consumers and producers to make decisions regarding price, quality and other relevant factors when buying and selling. This can lead to the misallocation of resources. **Symmetric information** is when all the relevant information is known by both parties. **Information asymmetry** occurs when some parties in a transaction have more information regarding the product than others.

Perfect knowledge is a theoretical concept where all consumers in a market are fully aware of price, quantity available and other relevant information for all products when making buying decisions.

1.3.4 Information gaps

Imperfect market information leads to a misallocation of resources in all real-world markets. Therefore, buyers should try to improve the situation by increasing the information that they have available:

- A seller of a second-hand car knows more about it than a buyer. To improve their knowledge the buyer could pay a mechanic to have a look at the car

- Mass advertising for the latest Hollywood blockbuster film persuades an individual to go and watch it at the cinema. They would be better informed by looking at reviews on independent websites

- Individuals looking for a job find it difficult to match their skills with vacancies. The government created a website (Find a job) to match those looking for jobs with available vacancies. This can be done by job and location

Market information can be improved, in order for it to become closer to being symmetric. However, this costs time and money. There is also a significant problem in that many economic agents do not want information to be symmetric. English philosopher Sir Francis Bacon is thought to have written the phrase "Knowledge is power". A supplier having more information than a buyer has a distinct advantage in a market.

1.3.4 Information gaps

1. Define the term "symmetric information".

2. Define the term "asymmetric information".

3. State two ways in which imperfect market information might lead to a misallocation of resources.

4. Why might the government provide information to a market?

5. Define the term "perfect knowledge".

6. Explain how perfect knowledge might lead to changes in the price and quantity sold of goods and services.

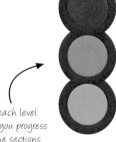

Tick off each level reached as you progress through the sections

1.4.1 Government intervention in markets

Government intervention

- The government intervenes in both the macro and micro economy. In a micro sense it will intervene in individual markets e.g. agriculture.

- To **reduce market failure** in order to:

    - Reduce or eliminate negative externalities

    - Increase or maximise positive externalities

    - Increase the supply of merit goods

    - Reduce the supply of demerit goods

    - Supply public goods that would be undersupplied by the market

- To **reduce inequalities** in the distribution of income and wealth:

    - Unequal distribution can lead to poverty

    - Tensions in society can be created

    - A breakdown in society can cause further market failure

1.4.1 Government intervention in markets

- To **support UK industry**:
- Full employment is a government target
- Some industries are more important as they employ large amounts of labour
- Infrastructure is essential if business is to provide quality services

To what extent should the government intervene?

Free market economists believe government should act as a 'shepherd' to ensure that a market follows the laws of demand and supply. Businesses should concentrate on supplying what is demanded. **Consumer sovereignty** means consumer choice will decide what to produce. **Laissez-faire**, meaning 'to leave alone', suggests government should only intervene to ensure free and competitive markets.

Interventionist economists argue that consumers need to be protected from exploitation by businesses. **Producer sovereignty** means that producers have the ability to use monopoly powers to decide what to produce and how much to charge. Without a competitive market consumers have little choice but to buy the products offered by these businesses.

1.4.1 Government intervention in markets

Governments influence the allocation of resources through:
Public expenditure: government spending to pay for the needs of society such as health, education and infrastructure.

Taxation and **subsidies**: making it more expensive for products that cause high negative externalities and cheaper for those that cause positive externalities.

Regulation: protecting consumers from the abuse of monopoly power that would lead to higher prices, supernormal profits and allocative inefficiency; creating an environment that will encourage firms to strive for productive efficiency through reduced costs.

Governments have a range of objectives and these affect how they intervene in a mixed economy to influence the allocation of resources.

Economic growth is a key objective as it leads to job creation, rising incomes, improved standards of living, international competitiveness, improved confidence, lower government spending and higher tax revenues.

1.4.1 Government intervention in markets

Reduced unemployment is a key objective as it leads to higher demand, higher incomes, improved standards of living, higher tax revenue, lower government spending, reduced poverty and social benefits such as reduced crime.

A low and stable level of Inflation is a key objective because it affects the value of money in your pocket, workers wage demands and consumer confidence. High, or rising inflation, damages the real value of money and erodes spending power. An inflation target of 2% has been set by the government. Reducing demand will impact on inflation but might lead to less spending on merit goods.

There are a number of ways in which governments can intervene to correct market failure. These include:

- Indirect taxation
- Subsidies
- Maximum and minimum prices
- Trade pollution permits
- State provision of public goods
- Provision of information
- Regulation

1.4.1 Government intervention in markets

Indirect taxation
Taxation is the medium through which governments finance their spending and control the economy. An indirect tax is a tax on a good or a service. A direct tax is a tax on an individual or an organisation. The incidence, or burden, of tax is the amount that the consumer or producer will pay for the tax.

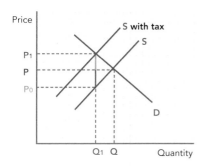

The imposition of an indirect tax will lead to an increase in the cost of supply for a firm. A **specific tax** is a set amount per unit. For example, a tax of 50p per fizzy drink. This will lead to a parallel shift in the supply curve. This will lead to a shift in the supply curve up and to the left. Quantity supplied will decrease by Q-Q1. Price will increase from P to P1. The incidence of the tax paid for by the producer is shown by the blue line, equivalent to P-P0. The incidence of the tax paid for by the consumer is shown by the green line, equivalent to P1-P. The revenue raised for the government by the tax is the distance from P0 to P1 multiplied by Q1.

1.4.1 Government intervention in markets

An **ad valorem tax** is a percentage of the price of the good or service. Therefore, the more expensive the product the greater the tax levied on it. An ad valorem tax will shift the supply curve upwards whilst also tilting it. As price increases the tax increases.

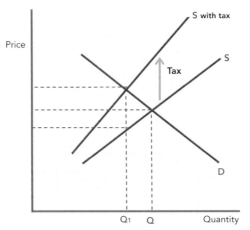

1.4.1 Government intervention in markets

Subsidy

A subsidy is a financial incentive to produce or consume a given product.

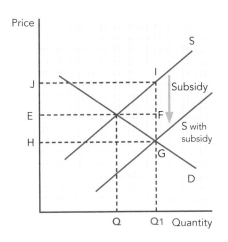

The imposition of a subsidy will lead to a decrease in the cost of supply for a firm. This will lead to a shift in the supply curve down and to the right. Quantity supplied will increase by Q-Q1. Price will decrease from P to P1.

The subsidy will be shared between the consumer and the producer.

1. Gain to consumers = EFGH
2. Gain to producers = EFIJ
3. Incidence of subsidy on government = IG
4. Government expenditure on subsidy = GHJI

1.4.1 Government intervention in markets

Maximum and minimum prices

A price control is when the government set maximum or minimum prices for a good or service.

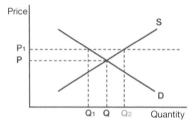

The imposition of a minimum price at **P1** will lead to excess supply of Q2 - Q1 as firms will wish to supply more at a higher price. The national minimum wage was introduced by the Labour Government in 1999 in an attempt to redistribute income to low paid workers. Some commentators suggested that the demand for workers would be lower than the equilibrium level and there would be an excess supply of labour.

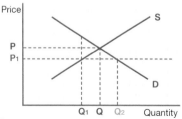

The imposition of a maximum price at **P1** will lead to excess demand of Q2 - Q1 as consumers will wish to demand more at a lower price. The government may wish to impose a maximum price to prevent the consumer from being exploited.

1.4.1 Government intervention in markets

Trade pollution permits

Pollution permits allow firms to produce a legal level of pollution every year. Permits are tradable on the market; if a firm does not use all of its permits it can sell them to other firms that pollute above their allowance. This provides a financial incentive for firms to reduce pollution. Trading schemes seek to reduce CO_2 emissions globally. However, it is difficult to assess the amount and level of permits to provide to firms.

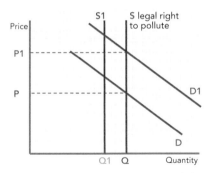

Government issue a fixed amount of pollution rights in the economy. Therefore, supply is perfectly inelastic as it cannot change. If there is an increase in demand for pollution permits (the legal right to pollute) demand will shift from D to D1 and the price of these tradable permits will increase. Firms will either pay more for the right to pollute or they will be incentivised to reduce pollution. Those who do not need their permits can sell them on the market.

Governments can enforce stricter pollution control by reducing the number of tradeable permits to Q1. This will lead to a shift in the supply curve to S1 leading to higher prices and a higher cost to firms of creating pollution.

1.4.1 Government intervention in markets

State provision of public goods
State provision occurs when the government, or state, intervenes in the market in order to supply a good or a service. This happens when goods and services are either:

- A merit good - the government supplies goods and services such as state education and health e.g. NHS as society believes that these are under provided by the market mechanism

- A public good - the government supplies goods and services such as defence and infrastructure e.g. roads as these would be under provided by the private sector due to the free rider problem

The government will intervene to ensure that an adequate supply of these products is available to the market.

1.4.1 Government intervention in markets

Provision of information
This occurs when governments seek to redress the problems caused by a lack of information. The greater the information available to consumers the more likely they are to buy goods and services with confidence. Government try to ensure that economic units can maximise decisions when consuming and producing goods and services by providing information where the private sector fails to do so. It provides information in a variety of areas e.g.

- The job market
- Dangerous products e.g. cigarettes
- Economic data to help firms plan for the future

Regulation
Regulation occurs when the government seeks to provide effective competition within markets. It is believed that this will protect the interests of consumers so that they are not exploited by firms. Regulation will lead to greater choice and lower prices. This takes place in a number of industries e.g. telecoms and energy.

1.4.1 Government intervention in markets

1. State three reasons why governments intervene in markets.

2. State three ways in which governments can reduce market failure.

3. State two reasons why governments might intervene to support UK industry.

4. Explain three methods of government intervention to correct distortions in individual markets. For each method use a diagram to illustrate your answer.

5. Explain, with the use of a diagram, how the imposition of an indirect tax can be used to increase government revenue.

1.4.1 Government intervention in markets

6. Explain, with the use of a diagram, how a subsidy can be used to increase the supply of goods and services to a market.

7. Explain, with the use of diagrams, how price controls can impact on markets.

8. Explain three methods used by the government to influence the allocation of resources.

9. Explain three government objectives and how these might affect the allocation of resources in a mixed economy.

Tick off each level reached as you progress through the sections

1.4.2 Government failure

Government failure occurs when government intervention in markets leads to a net welfare loss in comparison to the free market operating alone. The government create, rather than remove, market distortions leading to allocative inefficiency. Therefore, economic welfare is reduced, rather than improved and there is a **net welfare loss**.

Causes of government failure include:

Distortion of price signals
The government try to create incentives and disincentives in order to influence behaviour of both individuals and firms. This in turn, helps to create markets that would not survive in their present situation without government support. This distorts the free working of the market and creates distorted prices. This can lead to the government creating inefficiencies rather than correcting them.

1.4.2 Government failure

The law of unintended consequences

This occurs because unexpected events can occur due to government intervention. This will happen if consumers or producers act in a manner that was not foreseen by the government. This can lead to a worsening of the situation that the government was trying to create a solution for. For example, government might intervene in housing markets to control high rents. This would mean that landlords had to reduce rents. Some landlords might see this as a disincentive and withdraw their houses from the rental market. This fall in supply would actually aggravate the situation, making it harder for people to find rental accommodation.

Excessive administration costs

Administrative costs are the expenditures that the government spends on intervening in markets. Administrative costs can mean that the benefits derived from government intervention are outweighed by the costs. This can occur as government bureaucracy leads to higher costs. Budgets are constrained, particularly in times of recession because decisions have to be made on where to spend a limited amount of money. Often, incorrect decisions are made where the costs do not achieve the expected benefits.

Information gaps

Information used by government can be inaccurate due to poor research or inability to predict the future. This delivers the wrong signals to markets meaning decision-making is flawed.

1.4.2 Government failure

1. Define the term "government failure".

2. Explain how government intervention can result in a net welfare loss for society.

3. Explain how government intervention can lead to the distortion of price signals.

4. Define the term "the law of unintended consequences".

5. State three reasons why government intervention can lead to the law of unintended consequences.

6. Explain how administrative costs can mean that the benefits of government Intervention outweigh the costs.

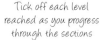

Tick off each level reached as you progress through the sections

The A Level Examination

Title (2 hours each)	Paper 1 Markets and business behaviour	Paper 2 The national and global economy	Paper 3 Microeconomics and macroeconomics
Themes	**Themes 1 and 3**	**Themes 2 and 4**	**Themes 1 – 4**
Marks (%)	100 marks 35%	100 marks 35%	100 marks 30%
Structure (All assessed by written exam)	**Section A:** MCQ and SAQ (25 marks)	**Section A:** MCQ and SAQ (25 marks)	**Section A:** DRQ - 25 marks; Essay – one from two (25 marks)
	Section B: 1 DRQ (50 marks)	**Section B:** 1 DRQ (50 marks)	**Section B:** DRQ - 25 marks; Essay – one from two (25 marks)
	Section C: Essay - one from two (25 marks)	**Section C:** Essay - one from two (25 marks)	

NOTES